WHY NOBODY
WANTS TO GO TO
CHURCH
ANYMORE

AND HOW 4 ACTS OF LOVE
WILL MAKE YOUR CHURCH
IRRESISTIBLE

Loveland, CO

Group

THOM & JOANI SCHULTZ

Group resources really work!

This Group resource incorporates our R.E.A.L. approach to ministry. It reinforces a growing friendship with Jesus, encourages long-term learning, and results in life transformation, because it's:

Relational—Learner-to-learner interaction enhances learning and builds Christian friendships.

Experiential—What learners experience through discussion and action sticks with them up to 9 times longer than what they simply hear or read.

Applicable—The aim of Christian education is to equip learners to be both hearers and doers of God's Word.

Learner-based—Learners understand and retain more when the learning process takes into consideration how they learn best.

Why Nobody Wants to Go to Church Anymore:
And How 4 Acts of Love Will Make Your Church Irresistible

Copyright © 2013 Thom and Joani Schultz

group.com | **lifetreecafe.com**

Credits
Editors: Jeff White and Candace McMahan
Assistant Editor: Kelsey Perry
Production Assistant: Cris Alsum
Cover Photo: Marcos Leal

Library of Congress Cataloging-in-Publication Data

Schultz, Thom.
  Why nobody wants to go to church anymore : and how 4 acts of love will make your church irresistible / by Thom and Joani Schultz.
    pages cm
  ISBN 978-0-7644-8844-3 (pbk. : alk. paper) 1. United States--Church history--21st century. 2. United States--Church history--20th century. 3. Church growth--United States. 4. Church renewal--United States. 5. Love--Religious aspects--Christianity. I. Title.
  BR526.S38 2013
  253--dc23
                          2013030541
10 9 8 7 6 5 4 3 2 1   20 19 18 17 16 15 14 13
Printed in the Unites States of America.

CONTENTS

Acknowledgements

Where to begin? God incredibly blesses us with amazing people who surround us every day.

We are eternally grateful for our parents, who raised us in the church and showed us Jesus. We especially thank our son, Matt, and his wife, Shawna, who bring such joy to us.

When it comes to our Group staff, we love them all and especially our awesome assistant Cris, who miraculously juggled our calendars, typed manuscripts, and double-checked source materials tirelessly till we accomplished our goal. Plus, Cindy Hansen, whose flying fingers typed the early stages of the manuscript.

This book and Lifetree Café would never have come into being without our "breakfast club of champions" (Rick Lawrence, Chris Yount Jones, Amy Nappa, Jeff White, Brian Abbott, Jody Brolsma, Jon Vaughan, and Rocky Gilmore) who continue to wade with us through the years of rigorous discussion, prayer, Scripture, and Fireside Café breakfasts. (Thanks Fireside staff!) It doesn't end!

Thanks to our Lifetree team, especially Craig Cable, Mikal Keefer, and Candace McMahan, who weekly immerse in this God-adventure we call Lifetree Café.

We are grateful for our friends in ministry who span all locations, faith traditions, and experiences—and our Lifetree Café friends who span all locations, faith traditions, and experiences.

And now thanks to the team who brought this resource into its multiple forms.

Kudos...

* to our word experts: Jeff White, Candace McMahan, Cris Alsum, and Kelsey Perry.

* to our production and marketing team: Amy Nappa, Becky Hodges, Melissa Towers, Jon Vaughan, and Amy Taylor.

* to our digital and media team: Brian Abbott, Brian Shumate, Matt Schultz, Shawna Schultz, and Four Story Creative.

* and the photos? All to Thom's credit, sharing his photography "hobby."

INTRODUCTION

THERE'S NO EASY WAY TO SAY THIS, BUT IT NEEDS TO BE SAID: THE AMERICAN CHURCH IS BROKEN.

Those words break our hearts more than you can possibly know. But before we jump into that subject—as well as the abundance of hope that things can change—you need to know our hearts. You need to understand why we care. And, most of all, you need to know how much we love the church.

Before we challenge you to change, to be vulnerable, it's only fair we reveal ourselves to you. It'll help you understand our perspective. In this book, we'll challenge you to take a "look in the mirror." Before we do, here's a peek at us. See if you can relate.

We both grew up in the church. We came from families that valued faith and churchgoing. And we've dedicated our lives to serving the church.

●   ●   ●

THOM: I grew up in a Christian home, the kind we hope kids today could experience. My dad taught Bible classes and held leadership positions in our churches. My mom was a pillar of prayer. I volunteered at church even as a junior high kid. God had placed something in my heart even then—both a love and an angst for the local church. As a teenager, I wrote a play called *Onward Christian Soldiers*, prodding the church to make changes. (Maybe some things never change…)

Through college and beyond, I volunteered as an adult leader for my church's youth group. That is, until I felt called to take a leap of faith and start Group Magazine, a meager little newsprint magazine filled with youth ministry ideas I thought others like me might desperately need.

With $500, prayer, and youthful naiveté, I started our company, Group Publishing. If I'd known then what I know now, I'd have known it couldn't be done. That's all the more reason we believe in God's miraculous power!

•   •   •

JOANI: My family story is a churched one, too. I served nearly 100 different churches for two years as a district "youth staffer." That included rural, suburban, and inner-city youth ministries. I stayed with families, lived out of my suitcase, and gained extra pounds because I was a "special guest" in host homes all over southern Minnesota. I can't believe I didn't even have an apartment! I consulted and served churches that desired my volunteer time. Just room and board—oh, and a $120 monthly stipend for toothpaste and sundries. What incredible hands-on, on-the-job experience!

For the next seven years, I loved serving fulltime at a church in Wisconsin wearing multiple hats—youth ministry, children's ministry…everything. I treasure my experiences there in an awesome team ministry with the pastor, Gene Glade, who remains a precious friend. The church allowed me to volunteer on regional and national levels, writing and planning events and leading workshops. Those amazing experiences and wonderful relationships prepared me for Group, which I joined when the company was 10 years old.

•   •   •

WE came together because of Group, which exists for one purpose: to serve the church. We got married as best friends, and at Group we've combined our faith, our love for the local church, our philosophy of what really works with people of any age, and our values.

We're regular people who've been on church staff and served as volunteers. We're happy to serve in the background, like accompanists, so your ministry can shine. We've dedicated our lives to serving the local church, while actively studying and immersing ourselves in the church.

We're passionate about the transformational power of a Jesus-centered life and God's desire for the church to embody that. Our goal is to see lives transformed.

Here's what else you need to know about us:

- **We love people in ministry.**

When we were growing up, our families were involved in our churches and supportive of our pastors. Thom's dad was the president of congregations; Joani's grandma was a widow and pastor's wife. When I (Joani) was growing up, we adopted pastors and their families. We'd invite them to meals and family events—they even helped us bale hay on our South Dakota farm. Both of us supported ministries as faithful volunteers. And today we enjoy entertaining people who visit Group headquarters when they attend ReGroups (intimate two- to three-day conferences). We love to open up our home so people in ministry can simply *be* as they get to know others who share their hearts for ministry in a warm, safe, comfortable environment. (And you're welcome to drop by Group anytime, be applauded when you walk in the door, and meet Bruce—our audio-animatronic talking moose!)

- **We're experience creators.**

We're not traditional publishers who only produce books. We hold tightly to our **R.E.A.L.** philosophy of learning:

Relational—Learner-to-learner interaction enhances learning and builds Christian friendships.

Experiential—What learners experience through discussion and action sticks with them up to 9 times longer than what they simply hear or read.

Applicable—The aim of Christian education is to equip learners to be both hearers and doers of God's Word.

Learner-based—Learners understand and retain more when the learning process takes into consideration how they learn best.

"Learning by experiencing" permeates all our Sunday school curriculum, vacation Bible school programs, books, magazines, online resources, training, mission trips, and more. "Do" is embedded in everything we do. We provide materials and experiences that immerse people in environments designed for them to encounter God and for their faith to grow.

First Corinthians 3:6-7 says, "I planted the seed in your hearts, and Apollos watered it, but it was God who made it grow. It's not important who does the planting, or who does the watering. What's important is that God makes the seed grow." The experiences we design are all about planting and watering.

7

- **Our organization serves the church.**

The hearts and attitudes of our staff reflect this in all their interactions with the people who buy our products. We don't call them customers—they're our friends in ministry. A great friendship includes time together, love, conversation, encouragement, and more. A true friend is also someone who will say the hard stuff. And sometimes the truth is tough to swallow. It's because we love our friends in ministry so much that we're willing to take the risk of saying difficult things. This book is an outgrowth of our love for the Lord, our love for our friends in ministry, and our love for people.

We talk with thousands of church leaders and workers every week. We live and breathe "church"—serving churches of every denomination, size, location, tradition, and ministry. Group is a safe, prayerful place for our friends in ministry to share their stories, both good and bad. Through those countless conversations, we've been able to keep our finger on the pulse of the church over the years.

We serve the majority of the reported 300,000 churches in North America in some way. Group materials reach more than 40 countries around the world. Millions of children, youth, and adults are recipients of our resources, whether they know it or not. Our resources work within the entire spectrum of Christian faith traditions. That's because we focus on what Christians agree on, not what separates us. (And there's a *lot* we Christians agree on—Jesus, for example.) We intentionally serve the span of Christendom, with the demographics of our churches matching the demographics of churches in North America within a few percentage points. Our team of more than 250 dedicated staff share in a united mission: *To equip churches to help children, youth, and adults grow in their relationship with Jesus.*

But as much as we love the church, we've found ourselves grappling with alarming changes in church participation and attendance in recent years.

For four decades, we've served in volunteer positions in local churches while working fulltime with Group. And we've loved seeing God at

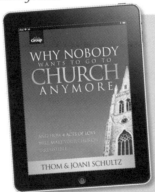

DIVE DEEPER into this book with the enhanced digital version! You'll get videos and links that give you a firsthand understanding of *Why Nobody Wants to Go to Church Anymore: And How 4 Acts of Love Can Make Your Church Irresistible.*

Find discussion questions, a forum to share feedback, and more at group.com/4-acts-of-love.

8

work through the church. But as time has gone by, we've grown weary of the politics and thankless hours as faithful volunteers. Sadly, we've found more and more worship services void of joy and fulfillment.

There is no shortage of books that beat up the church. This isn't one of them. But it does take a hard look at what's really working...and what isn't. We ask some tough questions...and demand honest answers. That's why we've set out on this expedition: to explore the real reasons people are leaving the church in droves—and what can bring them back.

> We never would have agreed to walk this path if we'd known where the guides were taking us.

We love exploration, so throughout this book we'll use some of our adventures around the world as parables to explain our ideas. Here's the first.

On a trip to Vanuatu (a group of islands in the Pacific) not too long ago, we found ourselves taking a journey into the unknown. Picture a completely black night in which you literally can't see your hand in front of your face. We rode inside a one-eyed pickup truck, lunging like a hungry bear over a rough road. The natives dropped us off near a stone-lined trail. We followed two lanky teenage guides wrapped in blankets to ward off the blustering wind. We hiked up, up, up...and then KABOOM! A deafening sound followed by an orange glow that lit up the rocky terrain around us. We were shocked to find ourselves standing inches from the edge of a boiling volcanic crater! We never would have agreed to walk this path if

9

we'd known where the guides were taking us. But now we would never trade that experience of witnessing the majesty and power of God's awesome creation. It was something very few get to experience—but there we were, toe to toe with one of the most powerful forces on the planet.

Willing to take the risk, we had followed our guides who'd been there many times before. And we lived to tell about it.

You're standing with us now on a similar edge. We may not be comfortable with the simmering cauldron beneath our feet. But if we're willing to face it—together—we'll get to explore something truly life changing.

10

1

THE PROBLEM IS WORSE THAN YOU THINK

It was clear
SOMETHING HAD GONE TERRIBLY WRONG.

A church in upstate New York had offered its building to serve as a home base for hundreds of teenagers. Youth groups from all over the Northeastern U.S. had gathered for a week of service to the local community. A buzz of excitement filled the air as the kids and their leaders worked hard, worshipped together, and grew closer to one another.

As the Week of Hope team showed us the grand old facility, we admired its beautiful architecture and stained glass windows. The pastor—a likeable, cheerful man with an indelible smile—noted that this was the most activity the church had seen in years. He admitted that the church itself wasn't nearly as alive as this tired but motivated group of teens. We sensed an underlying sadness. When we saw the preschool room, we learned it had been more than a decade since the little chairs were filled with children. Before long the pastor revealed the heartbreaking reality: Not too long ago, this church had been thriving with nearly 1,000 members. But now they were lucky to get 30 people to show up on any given Sunday.

There may have been no visible cracks in the stained wood and polished marble halls of this historic house of worship, but this church was crumbling before their eyes.

For updates on this church's story, visit group.com/4-acts-of-love.

This story broke our hearts. But what made it especially disheartening was that it was just one example of many. Shockingly, there are tens of thousands of similar stories about churches in various stages of stagnation or decline. *Perhaps as many as 200,000 American churches,* according to the latest statistics. Every year more than 4,000 of them close their doors forever.[1]

As sad as the story about this New York congregation may be, it's merely one small sign of an epidemic that's quietly and gradually sending the North American church into oblivion. Simply put, lots of people are leaving the church—many more people than you probably realize—and they're not coming back.

The problem is truly overwhelming. If you don't believe it, let us overwhelm you with some facts:

- Just over 350,000 churches dot the U.S. landscape. But only some small (less than 200) and some large (more than 2,000) churches are showing any growth. The vast middle is dwindling.[2]

- Churchgoers are getting older, on average, than the general population. The younger the generation, the higher the percentage that reports they are unaffiliated with a church.[3]

- Church attendance is shrinking. While 40 percent of Americans *say* they attend church every week, the actual number is more like 20 percent.[4]

- Four out of five Americans say they're sure God exists and identify themselves with a faith group. But less than half of them ever attend church.[5]

- Within five years, the percentage of congregations characterized by "high spiritual vitality" dropped from about 43 percent in 2005 to 28 percent in 2010.[6]
- In just five years, the percentage of teenagers attending church every week has dropped from 20 percent to 15 percent.[7]
- Giving is down in recent years—part of an ongoing decline.[8]
- In 2000, about a third (31 percent) of congregations exhibited "excellent" financial health, but by 2010 that number plummeted to 14 percent.[9]

- Every year, more than 4,000 churches close their doors compared to approximately 1,000 new (and mostly very small) churches that start.[10]

- Every year, 2.7 million church members fall into inactivity.[11]
- From 1990 to 2000, the combined membership of all Protestant denominations in the U.S. declined by almost 5 million members (9.5 percent) while the U.S. population increased by 24 million (11 percent).[12]
- Half of all churches in the U.S. did not add any new members to their ranks between 2010 and 2012.[13]

And all that's just the tip of the statistical iceberg.

WHY Does Nobody Want to Go to Church Anymore?

We've seen church people get tense, even angry, when we say, "Nobody wants to go to church anymore."

"Come on," they chide. "That's so negative. It's an exaggeration, and it's untrue. People still go to church."

True. A faithful few still do attend. But we're not the only ones taking notice of the alarming changes:

> Christianity itself is in crisis. It seems no accident to me that so many Christians now embrace materialist self-help rather than ascetic self-denial—or that most Catholics, even regular churchgoers, have tuned out the hierarchy in embarrassment or disgust. Given this crisis, it is no surprise that the fastest-growing segment of belief among the young is atheism, which has leapt in popularity in the new millennium. Nor is it a shock that so many have turned away from organized Christianity and toward 'spirituality,' co-opting or adapting the practices of meditation or yoga, or wandering as lapsed Catholics in an inquisitive spiritual desert. The thirst for God is still there. How could it not be, when the profoundest human questions—*Why does the universe exist rather than nothing? How did humanity come to be on this remote blue speck of a planet? What happens to us after death?*—remain as pressing and mysterious as they've always been?
>
> "That's why polls show a huge majority of Americans still believing in a Higher Power. But the need for new questioning—of Christian institutions as well as ideas and priorities—is as real as the crisis is deep.[14]

> The percentage of people that attend a Christian church each weekend is far below what pollsters report. According to both Gallup and Barna, 43% of American adults attend church on a typical weekend. But are people telling the truth about their behavior? Do people overestimate their church attendance when polled? Yes! The actual rate of attendance

14

from 'head counts' is less than half of what the pollsters report. Numbers from actual counts of people in orthodox Christian churches show that 18.7% of the population attended a Christian church on any given weekend in 2000.[15]

[The large megachurches mask the church's decline/death.] 'You have Joel Osteen's church with 20,000 or 30,000 people worshipping on an average weekend, and it just seems like religion is going great guns,' [Kirk] Hadaway says. 'I think it is creating a false impression of what is happening in the church. There are more giant churches now than there used to be—but at the same time, the average church is quite small. The decline among these small congregations has led to the death of a lot of churches. They have declining numbers and rising costs—insurance rates, pastors' salaries, utilities—making it really tough for many churches across America.'[16]

Young adults are leaving the church in record numbers, and experts wonder how many of them are ever coming back. LifeWay Research found seven in 10 Protestants ages 18 to 30 who went to church regularly in high school quit attending by age 23. A third of those had not returned by age 30. That means about one-fourth of young Protestants have left the church. The Barna Group says six in 10 young people will leave the church permanently or for an extended period starting at age 15. The 2012 Millennial Values Survey […] found college-age millennials are 30 percent more likely than the general population to be religiously unaffiliated. […] Just one in four says he or she attends religious services at least once a week, while 43 percent say they seldom or never attend. Nearly half of younger millennials still live with their parents, but those who live at home are no more likely to attend church than those who do not. […] Pollsters fear current trends signal more than sowing wild oats. […] Research suggests the main reason for disengaging from religion is […] their faith simply does not seem relevant or important to their daily lives.[17]

The church needs a wake-up call, just as we did.

THE PROBLEM IS **WORSE THAN YOU THINK**

Why Nobody Wants to Go to Church Anymore could have been titled *The Emperor Has No Clothes*. This book takes a deep, candid, and honest look in the mirror. And we may not like what we see.

It's like the shock when you open your eyes and see your body for what it really is. It's embarrassing. Maybe a bit disgusting. You feel ashamed that you let yourself go like this. You hope nobody's noticed. You sigh or gasp, grab that extra flab, and wonder, "What in the world has happened to me?" Jaron Tate, a contestant on *The Biggest Loser* likes to call it "sneaky fat." You wake up one morning and realize, "I don't look that good." Especially without any clothes on.

> You feel ashamed that you let yourself go like this. You hope nobody's noticed. You sigh or gasp, grab that extra flab, and wonder, 'What in the world has happened to me?'

Or maybe, like many people, you try to convince yourself that "I don't look all that bad. There are people worse off than me. Isn't there more to life than appearances, anyway? God only cares about what's on the inside, after all."

But, as we'll see, the inside isn't all that great, either.

> **NOW WE SEE THINGS IMPERFECTLY,** like puzzling reflections in a mirror, but then **WE WILL SEE EVERYTHING WITH PERFECT CLARITY.**
>
> —1 Corinthians 13:12

We, as the church, need to admit we don't look that good. When others see us, they're not all that attracted to us and wonder why we don't make some changes. For our own good—and for their good, too. But like those of us carrying around unhealthy poundage, we're looking for someone else to blame: McDonald's, Ben and Jerry's, potato chip manufacturers, giant sodas, commercials, oversized restaurant portions—hey, we're big-boned! Like the overweight, we in the church like to shift the responsibility to something or someone else: declining morality, Sunday sports, bad parenting, bad attitudes, lack of commitment, the media, technology, busy schedules, the economy, Satan, unstable global influences, the Internet....

Stop! Blaming gets us nowhere. And it's pointing fingers in all the wrong directions.

One thing we've learned at Group Publishing is to train all our leaders to speak the language of accountability. As a team, we read *The Oz Principle* together. It's all about building a culture of personal ownership and responsibility. We've learned a lot about how to address issues head on in a healthy, productive way.

The church must do this, too. And we've got to start by confessing that the church is broken.

Say it with us: "The church is broken."

We in the church have a "sneaky fat" problem. We really do. We need to admit it together, and we need to work on it together. We need to take ownership of the problem. We can point fingers, dig in, and try to convince ourselves it's not that bad. Or we can take action.

This book is for those who want to understand why nobody wants to go to church anymore. But most of all, it's for those who want practical solutions to *do* something.

We're not alone. God is with us—and the Holy Spirit wouldn't mind being our personal trainer.

First, we've got some big questions to answer:

* Even though more than 90 percent of Americans say they believe in God, why did most of them avoid church last weekend?[18]

* Why are nearly one in five Americans checking "none" for their religious affiliation—the fastest growing, highest-ever documented segment?[19]

17

- Why are researchers predicting that by 2020 more than 85 percent of Americans won't worship God at church?[20]

- If 88 percent of adults say their faith is important to them, why do the majority of them choose not to grow their faith in church?[21]

- Why are nearly two-thirds (64 percent) open to pursuing their faith in an environment that's different from a typical church?[22]

- Last weekend most people in America avoided church. And a sizable portion who did make it to church wished they were somewhere else. Why?

Pause here.

Let's take a long, hard look in the mirror. If you're honest with yourself, you may have had your own share of struggles, strife, questions, and doubts about the church you love, too. If so, you're like the thousands of church leaders we encounter every week.

If you're like us, it grieves you.

What This Book Is
REALLY ABOUT

So, why do we care?

The hard truth is that maybe we *all* blew it. Us, too. As a publisher of Christian education resources, we may have gotten it all wrong.

About 20 years ago, we wrote a book called *Why Nobody Learns Much of Anything at Church: And How to Fix It.* We wanted to be a catalyst to revolutionize Christian education. And to our great surprise, much of the landscape of the way the church teaches the Bible, especially to teens and children, changed. It worked! People of all ages began experiencing the Bible as they never had before. It was a mini revolution!

But we now realize our laser focus on education was a distraction. That's because faith is *not* a subject.

Faith is a *relationship*.

Those four simple words compelled us to write this book. Think about that for a moment. *Faith is a relationship, not a topic to be studied.*

Once we understood that, our view of what happens at church changed. Completely. And it's opening doors we never even knew existed.

Remember, we love the church.

It's God's idea, God's people, God's church. And it's not going away. But the hard, honest truth tells us that the American church is growing increasingly irrelevant. Our church has become something that's easy to ignore. It's become something that fewer and fewer people want to be part of.

We can't help but wonder what needs to be done to keep this ship from sinking or drifting into obscurity.

Join us in our journey of vulnerability and vision. We'll share what we learned when we took our own long, hard look in the mirror to discover why nobody wants to go to church anymore. And we'll explore some exciting ways that "4 ACTS OF LOVE" will make your church irresistible.

We've been astonished by what actually works.

You'll feel our angst and our joys as we had our ah-ha moments. We hope you have a few of your own along the way. And maybe, just maybe, you'll discover a renewed love and understanding for what the church—the bride of Christ—can really be.

We have a choice. We can stay the course and cling to the status quo...or we can choose to do something.

Let's do something.

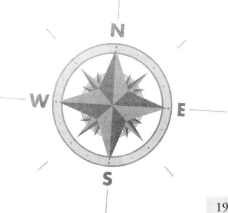

19

Endnotes

1. Scott Thumma, "A Health Checkup of U.S. Churches" by Hartford Institute for Religion Research (presentation, Future of the Church Summit from Group Publishing, Loveland, CO, October 22, 2012).

2. Ibid.

3. Ibid.

4. Ibid.

5. Ibid.

6. Ibid.

7. Ibid.

8. Ibid.

9. Ibid.

10. Steve Hewitt, "Why the church is dying in America," *Christian Computing Magazine*, July 2012, 3.

11. Ibid., 4.

12. Ibid.

13. Ibid.

14. Andrew Sullivan, "Christianity in Crisis," *Newsweek*, April 2, 2012, http://www.thedailybeast.com/newsweek/2012/04/01/andrew-sullivan-christianity-in-crisis.html.

15. David T. Olson, "12 Surprising Facts about the American Church" (presentation, Mission America Annual Conference, Kansas City, MO, 2007).

16. Bob Smietana, "Statistical Illusion," *Christianity Today Magazine*, April 1, 2006, http://www.christianitytoday.com/ct/2006/april/32.85.html.

17. Bob Allen, "Millennials losing their religion," Associated Baptist Press, June 25, 2012, http://www.abpnews.com/culture/social-issues/item/7555-millennials-losing-their-religion.html.

18. Pew Research Center, "'Nones' on the Rise," The Pew Forum on Religion and Public Life, October 9, 2012, 48.

19. Ibid., 9.

20. John Roberto, *Faith Formation 2020: Designing the Future of Faith*, (Naugatuck, CT: LifelongFaith Associates, 2010), 29, http://www.faithformation2020.net/uploads/5/1/6/4/5164069/ff_2020_chapter_1_-_8_driving_forces.pdf.

21. The Barna Group, "Americans Are Exploring New Ways of Experiencing God," June 8, 2009, http://www.barna.org/barna-update/article/12-faithspirituality/270-americans-are-exploring-new-ways-of-experiencing-god.html.

22. Ibid.

WHY NOBODY WANTS TO GO TO CHURCH ANYMORE

2

Is anyone in the church ASKING PEOPLE WHY THEY SKIP SUNDAY MORNING CHURCH?

We wondered.

It seems as if the church has forgotten the rest of the world, the "regular people." We don't get them. Mostly because they're not like us—or maybe they're more like us than we know.

Why don't they want to go to church anymore? Why are they going out for breakfast? Why are they playing sports? Why are they sleeping in? Why isn't church the priority it used to be?

We sure wondered.

So armed with a video camera and curiosity, we set out like detectives on a sunny Sunday morning in search of evidence. (Since we were usually in the pew on Sundays, we'd been oblivious to the growing numbers of non-goers.)

We simply asked people why they weren't in church. Here's what they told us:

- "I was raised to go every Sunday. I did the whole communion and confirmation, the whole nine yards. I guess I just decided that I could worship outside, too. I'm pretty spiritual, but I just kind of take it on a different level."

21

- "It's been quite awhile. I lost my wife about five years ago, so I don't do much. I'm retired. I just didn't bother to go. I don't have any good reasons."

- "A lot of them today are just so stiff and formal in their delivery and the structure of their sermons that I think the cliché of putting everybody to sleep is literally true."

- "The weekends become a time when the errands get done, the laundry gets done, the house gets cleaned. It becomes your only family time—the only morning you don't have to be somewhere. It's a time to sit down and have breakfast together. It's kind of hard to say to everybody, 'Get up, get motivated, get dressed,' like every other day."

- "[I don't like] having to be so quiet and get up early."

- "I was used to the passive, where you were preached to, you responded in a minimal fashion, and then you closed the door and went home. Nothing was ever said after."

- "Church can be a one-way discussion. In the church that I went to, even though I knew most of the people, it was so big there wasn't room for the people there to talk back. Too often it's just the minister [...] talking to you and not you talking to them."

- "I want the little church where everyone is a family and everyone cares about each other and everyone is sitting there learning about the Word without worrying about everything else. Everyone seems to just want to be bigger and better than the other church, and I don't think that's what church is about. It should be a place for fellowship."

Revealing, isn't it? We could fill this book with the reasons (*reasons*, not excuses) people say they don't go to church.

DO: Enlist a brave interviewer and camera operator. (A smartphone video will do just fine.) Head out on a Sunday morning and simply ask, "Why aren't you in church this morning?" Show and discuss your findings with your church leaders. Then take action by implementing some of the ideas in this book.

Over the years, we've continued to study culture, conduct research, and ask questions. After more detective work, hundreds of interviews, and years of listening, we began to realize that the reasons revolved around four recurring themes.

FOUR REASONS
Nobody Wants to Go to Church Anymore

1. "I feel judged."

A young woman told us that as a child she regularly attended church and Sunday school. But she's given up on the church as an adult. "They make me feel like an outcast," she said. "How? Why?" we asked. "Well, I'm a smoker," she said.

> 'Church people judge me.' According to their studies, 87 percent of Americans label Christians as judgmental.

Gabe Lyons' and David Kinnaman's groundbreaking research in their book *UnChristian* confirms the young woman's sentiment that "church people judge me." According to their studies, 87 percent of Americans label Christians as judgmental. And 91 percent say Christians are anti-homosexual, which we'd lump in the "judgmental" category.[1]

Fair or unfair, most people view the church as critical, disapproving, and condemning. Whether it's behavior, looks, clothes, choice of friends, lifestyle decisions, or whatever, the church has a solid reputation for acting as judge and jury over our individual differences.

23

Reflect on that for a moment. Have you ever felt judged by someone in the church? Chances are, you have. Probably more times than you'd like to admit. Maybe you didn't quite fit in. Maybe you said the wrong thing. Maybe you didn't look quite right. But you were judged (more likely misjudged) and it hurt, at least a little.

Let's be even more honest with each other. Have you ever formed negative opinions about people who came to your church? Maybe they didn't quite fit in. Maybe they said the wrong thing. Maybe they just didn't look right. But you came to your own conclusions about them, perhaps a bit unfairly. It's an easy thing to do, and we've all done it at some point or another.

Is it possible to create an environment where people are welcomed and accepted...no matter what they look like? No matter what they say? No matter what they believe? Is it possible for church to be the place where the average person can walk in off the street, warts and all, and be fully embraced? Is it possible for the church to become known as the least judgmental place Americans know?

We believe the answer is yes (but more on that later).

2. "I don't want to be lectured."

In other words, "You don't care what I think or wonder about."

More than ever, people today want to participate in the discussion. One man told us he's talked with more than a thousand other men who've given up on church. He said, "Guys don't want to sit in a room and idly listen to some preacher do all the talking. They want to ask questions. They want to share their thoughts, too."

They don't want another lecture.

Lyons and Kinnaman say two of the younger generations of adults want to converse: "Mosaics [those born between 1984 and 2002] and Busters [those born between 1965 and 1983] are the ultimate 'conversation generations.' They want to discuss, debate, and question everything. [...] Young outsiders want to have discussions, but they perceive Christians as unwilling to engage in genuine dialogue."[2]

We've found that all ages—from preschoolers to the elderly—want to engage in conversation. Think how un-conversation-friendly our churches are designed to be. Sitting in chairs or pews, facing a stage, and looking at the backs of people's heads is hardly conducive to talking with others.

And it's not just conversation people are after. They have questions. They have doubts. They have stories they want to share. They wonder about a great many things. But there's no place for their questions, their doubts, their stories, or their wonderings in church.

Instead of meaningful dialogue and engagement, the most common church experience today centers on the Sunday morning sermon. A lecture. A 30- to 45-minute speech. Yet even the most stirring oration doesn't build relationships. When was the last time you grew closer to someone because you both sat through a lecture together? It's no wonder fewer and fewer people are looking to the church to grow closer to God and others.

What people really want, more than anything, are real connections with real people. They want to know and be known by others. They want intimacy and rapport. They want friendship and support. They want relationships.

And remember, faith *is* a relationship.

Is it possible to create a church environment where people can fully expect to grow closer to someone every time they go? Is it possible for church to be known as the place where we all go to grow relationships? Is it possible for the church to become known as the friendliest place in America?

Again, we say yes. (Details to come.)

3. "Church people are a bunch of hypocrites."

This isn't a small minority talking. A whopping 85 percent make this claim, say researchers Lyons and Kinneman.[3]

We know, we know. Every church leader in America is weary of this "excuse." But people aren't merely referring to incongruous behavior. What bothers them is the sense that church leaders act as if they alone have all the answers. As if they've arrived. As if they're only interested in telling others what to do—"teaching," to use ministry vernacular.

We *are* a bunch of hypocrites. We're *all* guilty of saying one thing and doing another. We're all sinners. Romans 3:23 says, "*All* have sinned and fall short of the glory of God."

So when it comes to church, we can't keep pretending we've got it all together. We can't keep trying to put on a perfect face.

Think about what happens at a typical Sunday morning service. The congregation gathers into the holy sanctuary ready to worship. After a few songs and an announcement or two, the pastor takes the stage and gives a lecture—typically about how God wants us to live better lives. With rare exceptions, the pastor, along with a team of leaders, portrays an image of maturity, wisdom, and expertise—a living, breathing example of how awesome our lives could be if only we followed Jesus more closely. What's more, the tone of the sermon is commonly about how the congregation has fallen short.

Sure, there are exceptions. But the vast majority of church worship services project a sense of holiness that most (actually, none) of us can live up to.

Is the hypocrite label fair? Unfair? Does it really matter?

What matters is that people are staying away from church because they perceive it to be a place that insists on an impossible standard, which even its best leaders can't live up to. What matters is that people might—just might—come to church again if they could count on it to engage the realities of life.

Is it possible to create a church environment where people find genuine authenticity on every level? Is it possible for church to be known as the ultimate home for sincerity? Is it possible for the church to become known as the least hypocritical place in America?

As you'll soon find out, the answer can absolutely be yes.

4. "Your God is irrelevant to my life. But I'd like to know there is a God and he cares about me."

Most people don't experience God at a typical church service. They're not looking for the deep theological trivia that seems to interest a lot of preachers. They crave something rather simple. They want to be reassured that God is real, that he is more than a historical figure, that he is present today, and that he is active in the lives of people around them.

They don't understand that God *is* real and active in their daily lives. What evidence do they get of God at church? It's not through a sermon full of well-quoted Scripture and unrealistic platitudes. It's not with a handful of beautifully sung worship tunes. It's not because of a rigorous handshake at the door. And it's not from a plate passed around the room to collect their money.

We're not being cynical here. We, too, want to experience God in church. We, too, have struggled with finding the divine in the world around us. Like us, people want to follow Jesus.

Sadly, research by the Barna Group reveals that only 44 percent of people who attend church every week say they regularly experience God at church.[4] No wonder God doesn't seem relevant.

In a place where no one's allowed to ask questions, share doubts, engage in dialogue, or be completely honest, relevance simply can't exist.

People are spiritually hungry. People do want to grow closer to God. People are eager to find meaningful relationships. But people also have real concerns and issues that are never addressed in church. We're not sure churches can be relevant when they don't seem to be in touch with the raw, everyday lives of the community around them.

Relevance isn't the worship pastor showing his tattoo on stage. Relevance isn't serving fair-trade coffee in your lobby. Relevance isn't showing the latest popular movie clip during a sermon.

True spiritual relevance is seeing God in the matters at hand. Seeing God in *my* life.

Is it possible to create a church environment where people truly experience God all the time? Is it possible for church to be known as more in touch than out of touch? Is it possible for the church to become known as the most relevant place to go on Sunday?

Yes, yes, and yes. And yet…

OUCH!

When regular people hold up a full-length mirror in front of us, we don't like what we see. We don't like that we've been stripped like that fabled emperor. We certainly don't like that we've been strapped with such a poor reputation. But if we're honest, we have to admit that the "regular people" might have a point.

What if we, the church, acknowledged that we have to make some changes?

It's a lot like realizing that a healthy diet and exercise are our only hope. If we're willing to make some radical changes and be all that God wants us to be as the body of Christ, will the regular people start seeing us for who we really want to be—just other regular people created in the image of God?

Where Do **WE START?**

So what do people really want out of church?

Thankfully, researchers George Gallup, Jr. and D. Michael Lindsay have uncovered exactly that. Their extensive study uncovered…

27

6 Basic Needs of Americans

1. The need to believe life is meaningful and has a purpose.

2. The need for a sense of community and deeper relationships.

3. The need to be listened to and to be heard.

4. The need to feel one is growing in faith.

5. The need to be appreciated and respected.

6. The need for practical help in developing a mature faith.[5]

From the stories we've heard from thousands of people around the country, the average church service is not meeting these basic needs.

Make no mistake, people are longing for what Jesus offers. People may be leaving the church, but they're hungering for God. Consider these encouraging statistics:

- 91 percent say they believe in God.[6]

- 88 percent say faith is important.[7]

- 64 percent are open to pursuing their faith in an environment different from a typical church.[8]

People want God. Just not how the church packages God. They stand on the sidelines, watching Christians living their lives as though God doesn't really make a difference. Why should they waste their time?

A Church Staff Person Wonders

Some basic reasons for not going? It's someone telling you how to think; it's not real; it's a performance; it's too early; it's too nice outside; and I have better things to do. For my youth, the church seems fake, it's dying, it's not community, they can't ask questions, they can't live up to expectations—all judgment, no hope.

Why do they come to youth stuff? It is their community. They're accepted, loved, can ask questions, open discussions, and can explore God's Word together. There's no lights, camera, action. Just real people who aren't trying to make an impression.

For me, it's the same. No depth, no hope, no discovery. It isn't like the church in Acts. To me, the church has gone backward. As a staff person—it can be a hard place to work. I prefer real community, where people take care of each other and love each other for who they are.

— P.S.

The **POWER** of Experience

One of the first things we need to do is learn about the power of experience.

Church leaders have made some faulty assumptions from their own ministry practices. They assume that if they tell people what to believe, then that will result in the action of them becoming believers.

But that's not how it works.

Ever.

Our *experiences* actually form our beliefs, which then form our actions, followed by results.

For example, our family experiences shape our beliefs about family. Our school experiences shape our beliefs about school. If our experiences with church are legalistic and punitive, those experiences shape our beliefs about God. And those beliefs shape our actions and how we interact with the church.

How People
EXPERIENCE CHURCH

To get inside these four main reasons nobody wants to go to church anymore, it's helpful to explore why people feel this way about the church. We need to understand how we got here. In looking back, we will be able to move forward.

Because the church, at its core, is people who claim to follow Jesus, "regular people" perceive "church people" through what they've experienced in their interactions with church people. As usual, the power of experience reveals a lot.

The book *UnChristian* reminds us, "It is important to realize that young outsiders [and old outsiders, we might add] attribute their image of Christianity primarily to conversations and firsthand experiences. [...] They have had very personal experiences, frustrations, and hurts, as well as devastating conversations and confrontations. [...] The scars often prevent them from seeing Jesus for who he really is."[9] They've tasted what Christians offer in and out of church, and they don't like what they experienced.

A Trip Down
CHURCH STREET

It helps to visualize these experiences as various buildings along a city street. Perhaps "regular people" aren't connecting with the church today because they perceive it to be more like a police department, a political action committee, a theater, a mortuary, a seminary, or a museum.

Which one might describe *your* church?

The Police Department

Rules rule in police department churches. These churches make sure people follow a long list of do's and don'ts. Signage, bulletins, newsletters, websites, sermons—everything revolves around letting others know the rules. They've made the law and obedience their top priorities, or at least their most visible ones.

In a world of people desperate for Jesus, do we hope our God is most known for the 1,000 Commandments?

We all understand that certain rules are important. No one wants a world (or a church) governed by chaos. What would driving be like if there were no rules of the road? Rules and laws keep things orderly and safe.

But what's the main message your church is sending to the people who visit it? Do announcements remind people about the correct way to park in the parking lot? Are there signs all around the church building instructing people which doors not to enter, where to pick up children, and when to flush the toilet? Do sermons tend to focus on enforcing God's laws?

An easy way to tell if your church focuses too much on rules is to take a close look at your priorities. Do the signs on your walls communicate how much you love people...or are they more about keeping the building clean? Before you confront that guest about leaving a coffee cup on the table, ask yourself, "Do I care more about building a relationship with this person, or do I care more about the building?"

Let the police station be the police station. And let your church be a haven for thriving friendships.

Popular Church Rules

- how to baptize
- when to baptize
- which Bible translation to use
- when to observe the Sabbath
- what to eat and drink
- what to wear
- how to celebrate the Lord's Supper
- who may partake of the Lord's Supper
- which musical instruments (if any) are allowed
- what to do with candles, crosses, and flags
- how to address the clergy
- how to dress the clergy
- how women may serve in ministry
- when to stand
- when to kneel
- when to clap
- who can use the stuff in the kitchen

Walk, Don't Talk

Today I picked up our two young kids from vacation Bible school at a nearby church. I asked them what they learned. Without hesitation they said, 'When you're in a line, walk, don't talk. Look straight ahead and don't play around. When you get inside, sit quietly and don't talk or move.' Hoping for something a little deeper, I asked if they learned anything else. 'Yes,' they said. 'If you get up to go to the bathroom, you have to sit in the back and can't get back with your friends.'

— T.G.

> "And so the Lord says, 'THESE PEOPLE SAY THEY ARE MINE. They honor me with their lips, but THEIR HEARTS ARE FAR FROM ME. And their WORSHIP OF ME IS NOTHING BUT MAN-MADE RULES learned by rote.'"
> — Isaiah 29:13

The Political Action Committee (PAC)

Social action issues dominate the agenda and are the prime responsibility of these churches. The political process fascinates the leaders of PAC churches. But in a place that's supposed to foster relationships, they take a more political approach to everything they do.

The masses want spiritual growth. But PAC churches are feeding them a steady, force-fed diet of issues and action. Take a look at this list of PAC church priorities gleaned from a denominational magazine:

- a response to racism
- becoming more multicultural
- same-sex unions
- ordination of gays and lesbians
- sexuality studies
- poor and vulnerable populations
- federal child nutrition programs
- needs of elderly people
- church-wide evangelism strategy
- advocacy for people living in poverty
- world hunger
- refugee resettlement program
- protecting civil liberties of all people
- Israel and Palestine
- advocacy for foreign aid to Colombia
- international debt relief
- HIV/AIDS
- legalized gambling
- social statement on prisons
- war and peace

Of course, all these issues are important. We're not saying churches should never be involved in addressing some of the world's most pressing problems. (In fact, encouraging people to talk about issues like these can be a healthy, effective way to engage people and stay relevant.) But if these things are your main priority, then they're supplanting the need to let people experience God and grow closer to each other.

Churches should draw people together—not draw lines in the sand. As we'll see later in this book, it's entirely possible to bring people of many opposing viewpoints together who become lasting, supportive friends in the name of Jesus.

We once belonged to a congregation that had a great affinity for politics. Many of its members were quite experienced in local and state politics and issues. Ed, the associate pastor, devoted countless hours to community action projects.

When the senior pastor retired, the political activists launched a campaign-style blitz to promote Ed to the senior pastor position. His supporters set up petition-signing tables in the church entrance. They peppered the congregation with campaign mailings, complete with catchy slogans. They made campaign buttons and brochures.

Just before the congregational vote on the new senior pastor, the campaign committee promoted "Wear Red for Ed" Sunday. Ed's supporters, and Ed himself, came to church dressed in red—to sway voter opinion toward their "candidate."

He won. We left. They built a congregation in the image of a political action committee.

> "Jesus said, 'MY KINGDOM IS NOT OF THIS WORLD.' — John 18:36

The Theater

Theater lovers enjoy the stage. The stars. The spectacle. These churches deliver dazzling, orchestrated, crowd pleasing, seat filling, highly scripted, rehearsed shows. Even high-church, liturgy following traditions could be classified in the theater category. Everything is predictable. Today's megachurches have taken artistry, lighting, fog, technical wizardry, concerts, and other "wow" effects to new heights.

Are spiritually open people longing to watch someone on stage in a cleverly scripted world that frowns on flaws or technical difficulties?

More important, how in the world can relationships possibly grow in a performance-based atmosphere like that?

As a couple, we love the theater…in the theater. It's fun, and it's something we certainly enjoy. But we can honestly say that the theater of the church has never grown our faith or our relationship even the tiniest bit. It may be entertaining, but it's certainly not relational.

Again, let's remember: *Faith is a relationship.* The theater may be fun and enthralling, but it's *not* a relationship.

A Church in the Fog

I (Thom) asked our friends how things were going at their church. "We got tired of being in the fog," they said.

"I know how you feel," I said. "My church seems to have trouble finding its way through all the fog these days, too."

Our friends said, "No. That's not what we mean. We got tired of the fog. Real fog." They said their church had installed a theatrical fog machine. Every Sunday towering clouds of dense fog billow across the stage and spill into the audience.

"It's sometimes hard to see. And it's also hard to hear," they said. I wondered if the sound system was too weak. "No. Just the opposite. A lot of us complained the band is painfully loud. The pastor said we should wear ear plugs." So, now, as a ministry amenity, the ushers offer disposable ear plugs to arriving worshippers.

Every Sunday the crowds file into the darkened hall and sit in the fog with their ears plugged. The pastor stands in the lingering fog and delivers an entertaining monologue.

"On a Sunday morning, it's the best show in town," our friends said. They would know—they both have a bit of a theater background. "After all the years we invested in that church, we hated to leave. But it got to the point we couldn't see or hear God."

HolySoup.com

WHY NOBODY WANTS TO GO TO CHURCH ANYMORE

WHAT was Jesus after when he told the Pharisees the story of the two prayers? Luke 18:14 says, "For those who exalt themselves will be humbled, and those who humble themselves will be exalted." Jesus wasn't taken with the "show."

The Mortuary

Mortuaries have a certain smell. We can't quite identify it. But it's not a happy smell. It's a smell we've come to associate with solemnity. Mortuaries are serious places with muted colors. Subdued lighting. Quiet, pensive music.

Isn't it weird how some churches smell curiously like a mortuary? They're solemn, serious, and not fun. They stress (*embrace* is too cheery a word) the somber aspects of worship and faith. Mortuary mentality creeps in with music choices, traditions, and even their style of clapping (or lack thereof). Would people longing for an authentic life in Jesus look for it in a mortuary?

If ever a church were on the verge of passing into the great beyond, it's the mortuary-type church. Sure, mortuaries serve their place in the world, but it's certainly not where we go on a regular basis to grow closer to others. If you've ever been to one, you know exactly what we're talking about.

Churches should be places full of life and growth. They should be healthy harbors of hope, not gloomy graveyards of grief. Yes, there is a time for tears, but not every time we gather together. In Christ, we have so much to be joyful about!

Leaving in a Huff

I (Joani) grew up in a small, rural, tradition-filled church. It's hard to imagine, but there was a time when guitars were not in churches. Way, way back (we won't say how far back!) when I was a cutting-edge teenager, I stood in front of the church and led a worship song playing my guitar. One family stomped out and left that little church in a huff. They never returned. How could church be so sacrilegious?

35

> Jesus said, "For you are like whitewashed tombs—**BEAUTIFUL ON THE OUTSIDE** but filled on the inside with dead people's bones and all sorts of impurity. Outwardly you look like righteous people, but **INWARDLY YOUR HEARTS ARE FILLED WITH HYPOCRISY AND LAWLESSNESS.**"
>
> — Matthew 23:27-28

The Seminary

Seminaries serve a vital role as keepers of the facts. They are bastions for the transfer of knowledge. Academic rigor. Professor lectures. Tests. Debates. Research and in-depth study. Theological scholarship and doctrinal exactitude. Denominational seminaries guard the distinctions and advantages of their tribe. These institutes of divinity strive to ensure the accuracy of every jot and tittle of Scripture, teaching and drilling the intricate details of doctrine.

That. Is. Not. The. Church.

Is the church's primary role to transfer knowledge? *Of course* there is a role and a purpose for teaching. *Of course* we need to learn. But for the last few decades, the church has taken this priority to unhealthy extremes. *Teaching* the truth has become more important than *living* the truth. Churches have even adopted "fill ins" as a way for congregants to keep up with information delivered by their smart pastor.

Information is not the destination. If faith is indeed a relationship, then every church should focus on what it actually takes to grow that relationship.

Think about the people in your life who you're very close to. Did you grow your relationships with them by studying all the facts about their histories? Did you become more intimate because you memorized their genealogies and pored over all the letters, texts, and emails you've shared over the years? Did you learn the most about them by meticulously studying their pasts?

No. The way you grew closer was by spending time together. Eating together. Looking into each other's faces and talking about the things that matter most to you. You spent hour after hour together sharing your lives, listening, caring, and supporting each other.

Teaching and learning are merely one step on the road to transformation. That step goes somewhere, but the journey doesn't stop there. Relationships

36

with God and others are the key to growing in your faith. Can you imagine a church that centered everything on that foundation? We sure can.

Jeff, our friend and coworker, spent a year in Australia with his wife and kids on a teacher exchange. They discovered that the majority of Australians don't believe in God, yet they have a genuine curiosity about the Bible. That may be because Christianity has become a subject in schools there—just like geometry or biology. Jeff's wife, Amy, thought it was interesting that her students found God to be nothing more than a topic to be studied. The idea of faith as a relationship was a foreign concept to them. Let's pray that doesn't happen in America!

Holy Soup | Challenging the status quo in church with innovative approaches to ministry.

Holy Soup | Challenging the sta...   ☆ ▽ C Google

holysoup.com   POSTS

Most Visited ▾ Remedy Ticket Timecard GroupDrive Barcode Generator
              ABOUT   CONTACT   GET NEW POSTS BY EMAIL

follow Thom: f t ✉

Communication   Leadership   Learning   Outreach

Sermon Fill-in-the-Blanks Are _____.

Stupid. Yup, I (Thom) am afraid those fill-in-the-blank sermon outlines are simply stupid.

Obviously, that's not the intent. Those who use fill-in-the-blanks do so with good intentions. They say filling in blanks keeps listeners engaged and helps them remember what they hear.

Trouble is, these assumptions are problematic. While some people may enjoy monitoring sermons for missing words in an outline, many others find the hunt for mystery words actually distracts from the heart of the message.

And what's the evidence that fill-in blanks lead to higher retention and/or life application of a message?

If fill-in-the-blanks really worked, you'd use them everywhere. You'd hand out fill-in-the-blank papers to your children: "Don't forget to pick up your _____ and put them in the _____." You'd issue fill-in-the-blanks to your new office workers: "You'll find the printer ink in the _____ on the _____ side of the _____ room."

You know that wouldn't work. It's stupid.

What's more, use of fill-in-the-blanks sends troubling hidden messages. If you agree our chief ministry goal is to help people grow in relationship with the Lord, what do fill-ins imply? If you were pursuing a real relationship with another person, would you use fill-in-the-blank handouts?

I'm afraid fill-in-the-blank outlines diminish the nurture of a love relationship to a tedious academic exercise or a distracting puzzle.

So, a few recommendations:

1. If you wish to send people home with key thoughts on paper, simply provide them—without the silly blanks.

2. If you wish to accommodate people who like to take notes, simply give them a blank sheet of paper. They'll note key thoughts that matter to them.

3. If you wish to truly engage and involve your people, follow Jesus' examples. Let the people do some of the talking. Encourage questions. Use active experiences.

We're not here to play theological Trivial Pursuit. We're here to build friendships with Jesus.

In a world craving a transformational life in Jesus (even if they don't articulate it), the arrogance of information overshadows transformation. Faith is not a subject. Faith is a relationship.

P.S. See how others responded to my (Thom's) blog post at *HolySoup.com*. It will _____ you.

37

Only One Expert?

Some years ago a fresh, young seminary graduate arrived to pastor a small church in South Dakota. He was determined to share his "superior knowledge" with these "simple folk."

The women of the church invited the pastor to their weekly home Bible study. He agreed—but with one condition: that he alone would share any Bible insights.

So the women sat week after week and quietly listened to the pastor's knowledge. But they soon realized they weren't growing. "We always got so much more out of the Bible studies when we could share our own thoughts," one said.

These plucky women reached their limit when the young pastor proclaimed that Jesus intended the Great Commission for clergy only. He left the congregation shortly thereafter. And the ladies went back to pursuing Jesus.

> For it is written: '**I WILL DESTROY THE WISDOM OF THE WISE**; the intelligence of the intelligent I will frustrate.' Where is the wise person? **WHERE IS THE TEACHER OF THE LAW?** Where is the philosopher of this age? Has not **GOD MADE FOOLISH THE WISDOM OF THE WORLD?**
>
> — 1 Corinthians 1:19-20

The Museum

Museums remind us of days gone by. They exist to preserve the memories and traditions of the past. Some old cathedrals in Europe have become just that. Tradition can be useful, but when churches cling to "the way it's always been," we shouldn't be surprised that people today view church as outdated and archaic.

When tradition becomes a church's one thing, the church dies. Museum curators in the church cling to all sorts of "artifacts":

- music
- worship styles
- architecture
- furniture
- schedules
- versions of the Bible
- teaching and curriculum
- preaching styles (perhaps even preaching itself)
- the content of membership classes
- annual events

...and on and on.

Like relics in a museum display, these things sit unchanged for decades, doing nothing to nurture relationships with God and other people.

It's also important to note that traditions can become entrenched very quickly. Even within a matter of months, a church can develop and cling to new traditions that get in the way of growing real relationships.

Museums can be fascinating places to recall a bygone age—to stop for a moment and remember the impact of certain things, people, and events in our lives. But that moment shouldn't be the only moment we experience week after week. Our faith needs much, much more.

Ban the Coffee in the Entry

The worship committee at a church in our hometown discussed how to make the church more inviting. The team noted that people arrived just before worship began and left immediately after the service concluded. Few loitered in the lobby to talk, meet friends, or form relationships.

So the committee decided to place a coffeepot in the lobby to encourage people to stick around and enjoy some Christian fellowship. The plan worked. The aroma of fresh coffee lured people to the coffeepot. Once they grasped a cup, they tended to hang out, meet people, greet visitors, and talk with friends. The lobby started to become a warm gathering place.

But stop. The church's museum curators became inflamed. Coffee in the entry? This had never been done! This must be wrong. It must be sinful!

The final straw came when a curator spotted someone slip into the sanctuary with a cup of coffee. That was it. The elders called a special, secret meeting at 6 a.m. the next Monday. They voted unanimously to outlaw the coffeepot.

They sent word to the worship committee: "People can drink their coffee in the basement, like they always have—but not in the entrance to the house of the Lord!"

Take a moment to consider which stop along the street most describes your church. Be completely honest with yourself.

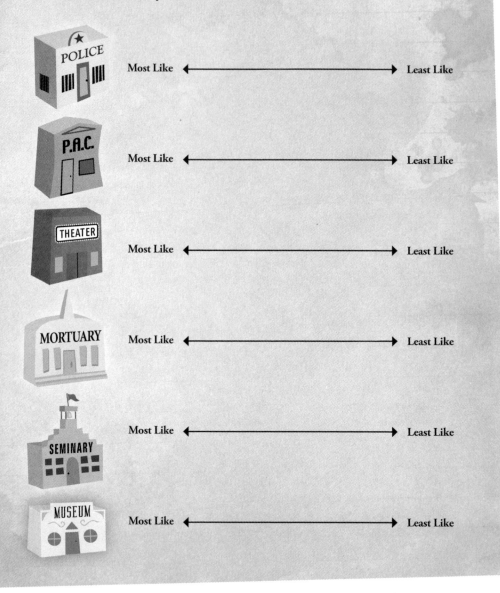

Because of these "streetscape" experiences, many people have left the church. We call them the church "declined"—those who've already voted with their feet. But not everyone has walked away. Some people feel very comfortable with the status quo. We call them the church "inclined."

The Church "INCLINED"

Since most people don't go to church anymore, who are the people in the minority who do regularly attend and appreciate weekly services?

Some have connected with churches that already embrace the 4 ACTS OF LOVE we'll discuss later. These fortunate few are already experiencing the richness, depth, and heart-altering practices of those churches.

But, sadly, most who appreciate church aren't in those churches. Instead, they fit a very specific profile. This shrinking minority—the church "inclined"—differs from the majority in several ways:

A **udience-Oriented.** They appreciate a good presentation from the stage. They prefer to listen passively while the paid professionals on stage do the work. Similar to theater-goers, they may judge the "performance" based on how well they are entertained or engaged.

A **nonymous.** They often seek anonymity. They like being part of a faceless crowd. They don't necessarily want to be noticed—or known. They appreciate churches that keep the spotlight on the performers on stage and allow the audience to sit quietly in the dark (literally and figuratively).

A **uthority-Centered.** They rely heavily on the official experts for information and inspiration. In the contemporary church, they count on the paid professionals to communicate the insights, move them, pray on their behalf, and do the real ministry.

A **cademic.** They see the church's role as primarily educational. They come once a week to obtain information about the Bible or God or life. They expect to hear an authority teach theological principles and historical data.

A **uditory.** They're often auditory learners—people who take in and remember primarily through their ears. The contemporary church service suits them because it's predominately an auditory experience (listening to music and lecture).

For the church "inclined"—or "reclined," as the case may be—this type of church experience satisfies them. This shrinking minority is content with the status quo.

41

The Church **"DECLINED"**

But what about the growing majority of people who don't regularly attend church services? Why don't these same factors work for them? It seems that what attracts the church-inclined may actually repel the majority or at least leave them uninterested. Let's look at each factor again from the church "declined" perspective:

NOT **A** **udience-Oriented**. Though most people enjoy a good show, they don't view their spirituality as a spectator activity. Even though they may long for God, they say they don't see the need to sit in an auditorium and watch professional religious people perform rehearsed presentations.

NOT **A** **nonymous.** People may seek occasional anonymity, but when it comes to matters of the heart they *crave relationships*. They want to be known. They want to contribute to the conversation. Telling their story is as important as listening to someone else's.

NOT **A** **uthority-Centered.** Most people today have moved into the new era of easy-access information made possible by the Internet. People no longer have to wait for authorities to deliver needed information. They're comfortable retrieving and processing it themselves.

NOT **A** **cademic.** We live in an information-soaked world. When it comes to spiritual things, most people don't sense they're lacking hard data. They're lacking the soft stuff of the soul. Their desired relationship with God seems more at home at Starbucks than in a lecture hall. Like any relationship, they sense that growth in a relationship with God comes more from give-and-take than passive consumption of someone's lecture.

NOT **A** **uditory.** Research shows that 30 percent or less of the population is made up of auditory learners. Most of the population processes information and thoughts primarily in other ways. They tend to tune out when asked to endure a presentation that implies they should sit still and listen.

Let's be clear: These people aren't uninterested in God or spiritual things. They simply don't find their experience with the church's common format to be a good fit for them. The typical Sunday morning service of half lecture and half sing-along isn't a useful way for them to connect with God.

It doesn't matter how carefully the preacher prepares or delivers the sermon or how well the musicians perform. *That formula just doesn't work for most people anymore.*

If today's church wants to reach beyond the shrinking church-inclined attendees, it will need to consider new and different ways to engage people.

We're not suggesting the church erase what it's doing for the current audience. Keep serving the church-inclined. But it's time to add some new experiences. At different times. In different environments. To grow the church. To be the church.

The **PIBOS**

There's also a group we call PIBOs.

They quietly walk into church, say little, look a bit detached, and leave quickly when the service concludes.

These church attendees are **P**resent **I**n **B**ody **O**nly (PIBO). They may be counted as members of a church's flock, but their hearts, minds, and souls are not engaged by what's happening at church. They are among the legion of people who, according to George Barna, never experience God at church. They attend out of a sense of duty, or to accompany a family member, or simply out of habit. For PIBOs, the church worship experience—even at grandly produced services—is a spiritual yawn. The worship recipe (half upfront monologue and half sing-along) does not stir the PIBOs.

Many church leaders may not recognize these people as PIBOs—or even care that their hearts and minds are not in the room. Because PIBOs satisfy the measurement that many leaders track—head count—they serve their purpose just as they are.

10 Wishes of a Pew Sitter

1. Banish the "stand and greet your neighbor" time in the worship service. I know your intentions are good but it's forced, fruitless, and goofy.

2. Forget everything they taught you about three-point sermons. You're wildly successful if you can get across one point. Just one point. Then sit down.

3. Get out and spend time with real people. Schedule lunches at your members' workplaces and schools. Listen. Get a feel for how real people live.

4. Encourage regular evaluation. Use comment cards. Ask us what we remember from last week's sermon. Then take us seriously and adjust.

5. Crank down the volume of the band. Allow us to actually hear the voices of the flock.

6. Burn the fill-in-the-blank sermon guides. They're insulting, distracting, and ineffective. (Can you imagine Jesus using them? Let's see, "Feed my _____.")

7. Show hospitality. Encourage people to enjoy a cup of coffee—during the service.

8. Let us participate. Entertain our questions—during the service. Let the real people around us share how God is working in their lives.

9. Relax. Make some real friends. Spend more time with your family. Don't schedule every evening with church meetings.

10. Get rid of the pews. Really.

NOW What?

Read what Alan Hirsch and Michael Frost wrote in *The Shaping of Things to Come:*

> All the tinkering with the existing model of church that's going on will not save the day. Simply making minor adjustments like replacing pews with more comfortable seating, or singing contemporary pop songs instead of hymns will not reverse the fundamental decline in the fortunes of the Western church. If you think of the church as a car, we cannot simply take it in for service. We need a whole new model. Or think of the church as a VCR. If you have newer DVDs, you can't play them on your old VCR—you need an entirely different device.[10]

Amen. We agree. So...

With all this swirling around us, we decided to take action. Like Queen Esther, we sensed God's call "for such a time as this."

What if, instead of the church being like a theater, a police station, or a seminary, it was more like a coffeehouse?

The rest of this book reveals our story—our bold new experiment that forever changed the way we think about church.

> What if, instead of the church being like a theater, a police station, or a seminary, it was more like a coffeehouse?

Endnotes

1. David Kinnaman and Gabe Lyons, *UnChristian* (Grand Rapids, MI: Baker Books, 2007), 27.

2. Ibid., 33.

3. Ibid., 27.

4. The Barna Group, "What People Experience in Churches," January 9, 2012, http://www.barna.org/congregations-articles/556-what-people-experience-in-churches.html.

5. George Gallup, Jr. and D. Michael Lindsay, *The Gallup Guide: Reality Check for 21st Century Churches* (Loveland, CO: Group Publishing, 2002), 12-14.

6. Pew Research Center, "'Nones' on the Rise," The Pew Forum on Religion and Public Life, October 9, 2012, 48.

7. The Barna Group, "Americans Are Exploring New Ways of Experiencing God," June 8, 2009, http://www.barna.org/barna-update/article/12-faithspirituality/270-americans-are-exploring-new-ways-of-experiencing-god.html.

8. Ibid.

9. David Kinnaman and Gabe Lyons, *UnChristian* (Grand Rapids, MI: Baker Books, 2007), 31-32.

10. Alan Hirsch and Michael Frost, *The Shaping of Things to Come* (Grand Rapids, MI: Baker Books, 2003), 34-35.

3

A BOLD NEW EXPERIMENT

Have you ever awakened and realized there was something so fundamental, so basic, that **YOU COULDN'T BELIEVE YOU'D MISSED IT ALL THESE YEARS?**

Maybe that's what's happened to the church. When we take a hard look in the mirror, we must confess: Our churches "talk" love, but we don't really "do" love.

Even a newborn baby knows love. Regardless of age, income, education, gender, or ethnicity—humans know and need love. We were created out of love to love, to be in relationship with our creator, God, and with each other. When we experience love, we experience God. We get a taste of the divine, the Source of Love. And that happens on Earth as people become the conduit for God's love to flow.

Jesus reminds us that the greatest commandments are to love God and to love our neighbors as ourselves (Matthew 22:37-39).

Look in the mirror again. Our churches "talk" love, but we've forgotten that what we *do* is more important than what we *say*. Actions always speak louder than words.

Faith Is a
RELATIONSHIP

We believe faith in God develops much like other relationships. That means it's rarely a strict, linear process. It's like relationships with other humans—messy, non-sequential, filled with ups and downs and

> We judge ourselves by our intentions, but others judge us by our actions.[1]

lots of forwards and backwards. Sure, a relationship includes knowledge and information, but that's not what makes a relationship tick. God can't be reduced to theological nit-picking and theoretical musings. God is real, alive, active in our world, and ultimately relational.

So, faith is a relationship with the living God...

who is real...

who reveals himself in Jesus...

who, through the Holy Spirit, reveals himself in people today.

Faith comes to life through relationships—loving God and loving others.

Missing the Guy in the Empty Chair

We're producing a generation of spiritual dwarves. Many in the church are going through the motions, but their faith lacks vibrancy, exuberance, life, and contagion.

They may be saying the right stuff. Doing the right stuff. But they're missing the main thing.

Yesterday, I (Thom) met a man who gets it. He introduced me to an empty chair. At least, it seemed empty.

His name is Wally Armstrong. He's a PGA golfer, author, and friend of Jesus. He wrote a book called *Practicing the Presence of Jesus*.

He explained how individuals and churches so often miss the main thing: a true friendship with Jesus. He said, "Either we are caught up in a flurry of performance as we try to live the Christian life in service to God, or we set our minds on acquiring more knowledge in the hope that with wisdom we will gain holiness. Of course, both of these paths leave us empty, because we've overlooked what Jesus came to give us."[2]

Armstrong described how, after spending decades hearing about Jesus in church, he chose to look at Jesus in a fresh, new way. He chose to imagine Jesus as a present, contemporary friend—a companion. He pictured Jesus sitting in a chair beside him.

It transformed his prayer life and his entire relationship with Jesus. He positioned an empty chair in his den. "I began picturing my Friend sitting across from me in the chair and myself talking to him," he said.[3] The chair experiment, as he calls it, helped to bring him "into the fullness of life and the companionship Jesus had always promised."[4]

This is the Jesus we're missing. This is the dimension of faith we're ignoring.

Our ministry methodology so often camps only on teaching about Jesus, drilling on biblical facts, and parsing theological nuances. Or we concentrate on coaxing our people to work—volunteering at church, serving in the community, doing good deeds.

Please understand. Knowledge is good. Service is good. But these are not the essence of faith.

Faith is not an academic subject.
Faith is not a list of do's and don'ts.

Faith is a relationship.
A friendship.
A companionship.

Maybe it's time to pull up a chair.

HolySoup.com

When it comes to finding clarity of purpose, we love Jesus' encounter with Mary and Martha. Jesus told the sisters that "only one thing" truly mattered. That "one thing" was exemplified in *the relationship being nurtured between Jesus and Mary.*

That's it. That's the one thing. The big deal. It's *relationship* that drove Jesus' ministry. And it's what he prepared his disciples to replicate.

Jesus showed that growing a relationship with him resembles how we grow a good relationship with other people. But he was criticized for that.

49

The religious elite called him a "glutton and a drunkard, a friend of tax collectors and sinners" (Matthew 11:19).

But his mission was clear. It was all about the relationship—with him and with others. That mission dominated everything he did and said. Building the relationship was more important than tradition. More important than formality. More important than religious taboos, such as picking grain on the Sabbath.

It's that devotion to relationship that drives our passion to relate better with those who do not yet have a relationship with Jesus, as well as those who have left it behind.

So what does a Jesus-centered, relationship-oriented church look and sound like? A very smart and talented guy named Paul said it best:

"If I could speak all the languages of earth and of angels, but didn't love others, I would only be a noisy gong or a clanging cymbal."

How many intelligent theologians, academicians, teachers, and preachers can impress the masses with silver-tongued oratory? But if listeners walk away without experiencing love...

"If I had the gift of prophecy, and if I understood all of God's secret plans and possessed all knowledge..."

How often have we been lured by three-point sermons, elaborate or simple strategies, clever acronyms, how-to books, and seminars? But if learners walk away without love...

"And if I had such faith that I could move mountains, but didn't love others, I would be nothing."

Has love gotten lost in an ever-increasing pile of to-do lists, comparisons, guilt, inadequacies, and shortcomings?

"If I gave everything I have to the poor and even sacrificed my body, I could boast about it; but if I didn't love others, I would have gained nothing" (1 Corinthians 13:1-3).

Social justice, wars on poverty, service projects, good deeds...sacrificial living might make us feel good about ourselves, but without love...

So What Does a **LOVING, JESUS-CENTERED, RELATIONSHIP-ORIENTED CHURCH DO?**

When people experience your church, do they find…

PATIENCE?
Almost All the Time ←——————————————→ Rarely

KINDNESS?
Almost All the Time ←——————————————→ Rarely

AN ABSENCE OF JEALOUSY?
Almost All the Time ←——————————————→ Rarely

AN ABSENCE OF COMPARISONS OR COMPETITION?
Almost All the Time ←——————————————→ Rarely

AN ABSENCE OF PRIDE OR EGOS?
Almost All the Time ←——————————————→ Rarely

AN ABSENCE OF RUDENESS OR PEOPLE DEMANDING THEIR OWN WAY?
Almost All the Time ←——————————————→ Rarely

AN ABSENCE OF IRRITABILITY?
Almost All the Time ←——————————————→ Rarely

AN ABSENCE OF A RECORD OF WRONGS?
Almost All the Time ←——————————————→ Rarely

AN ABSENCE OF GRUDGES?
Almost All the Time ←——————————————→ Rarely

AN ABSENCE OF REJOICING OVER INJUSTICES?
Almost All the Time ←——————————————→ Rarely

REJOICING WHEN TRUTH WINS OUT?
Almost All the Time ←——————————————→ Rarely

PEOPLE WHO NEVER GIVE UP?
Almost All the Time ←——————————————→ Rarely

PEOPLE WHO NEVER LOSE FAITH?
Almost All the Time ←——————————————→ Rarely

HOPE?
Almost All the Time ←——————————————→ Rarely

> People weren't hungry for fancy sermons or organizational polish. They just wanted love.[5]

> Christians *love* to use the excuse of the devil. It is the devil trying to rob you; it is the devil who has allowed this pastor to hurt you; it is the devil who comes to destroy…No one ever says the truth. The truth is when we're going about hurting others, we are not marked by love; and if we cannot operate in love to the underdog or porcupine, than we don't *know* him who is love. We are just a sack of religious garbage. We don't have revival because we crave being religious because really living for Jesus requires a change and sacrifice.
>
> — D.A.

What If We Really
BELIEVED THE TRUTH ABOUT LOVE?

Here's the most astonishing, freeing, scary thing: "Love never gives up, never loses faith, is always hopeful, and endures through every circumstance" (1 Corinthians 13:7).

What would happen if we really believed that?

What if we (Thom, Joani, and our team at Group) took a leap of faith, hope, and love and harnessed our God-given talents and the passion for the church we've lived for a lifetime—and poured it into a God-given dream for the church?

OUR BOLD (and Scary) EXPERIMENT

You know God is up to something when he wakes you up in the middle of the night. Isn't that what happens in the Bible? That's what happened to me (Thom).

It came as a waking jolt, not as a dream. I awoke at 3 a.m. with a commanding concept in mind. It was a wild idea for a time and place where people could gather and talk about life. God would be part of the conversation. These guided conversations would take place all over the country at the same time on the same topic. I didn't understand the idea, what it would look like, or how it would work. It was just a fuzzy, waking jolt.

Over time, a radical concept unfolded. God helped us weave our years of serving the church into a unique concept for "such a time as this." Like a reluctant Esther intent on saving her people, we began to experiment with the concept we would eventually call Lifetree Café.

Here's what God had given us to work with:

- decades of experience as a company that knows and loves the church,
- what we already know about the transformative power of R.E.A.L. learning (find the definition of R.E.A.L learning in the introduction to this book),
- mountains of research on church, generations, and culture,
- a love of adventure and risk,
- a desire to change the world,
- a talented team,
- a childlike faith that the same power that raised Jesus from the dead is working in us,
- a passion to live out the commandment to love God and others, and
- an openness to fail.

So like good "church people" we formed a committee. Well, not exactly. We challenged a small group of "Groupies" to meet at least once a week for breakfast, Bible study, and prayer for more than a year.

53

We ate scrambled eggs, yogurt, and granola. We guzzled cups of coffee and juice. And every time, we grappled. We uncovered everything we could about the status quo of churches, cultural trends, creative thinkers' ideas, what was working, and what was not. We prayed for guidance and God's insights. We met to wrestle, question, and wonder.

NOW WHAT Do We Do?

After all that grappling, we proposed a concept we believed would reach the ever-growing, non-churchgoing population. We decided to bring others into our fledgling think tank. We invited a small team of church-inclined and church-declined—all sharp thinkers who would tear apart our ideas. And that they did.

The good news?

We discovered that people outside the church aren't opposed to God. They're just suspicious and tired of the way church (as we know it) has been packaged. We heard from those who reject church. We respected their input.

Finally, after meeting for well over a year, one exasperated team member stood up and exclaimed, "Let's just do it!"

We all jolted awake like dead batteries come to life. He was right. Like the church we so desperately were trying to change, we'd become paralyzed. How did that happen? We realized how easy it is to wallow in information overload and fear. It was time to step out in faith and give birth to something new, bold, and a little bit scary.

Birthing PAINS

Things didn't start out so well.

Our hands got dirty. We made tons of mistakes. The process was messy and slow. We prayed for patience and help. We took every opportunity to learn from our mistakes and refine our idea. And there was no shortage of things to keep us humble.

Take our very first Lifetree Café event, for example.

We'd carefully planned an hour of experiences designed to foster conversation that would create an environment for God to show up. Well, he did, but not in any of the ways we'd expected. Our theme, "Give thanks in all circumstances," would prove to be an all-too-timely message.

It was a Sunday at 6:30 p.m. We met around small tables in the café at our headquarters. One of our team members had enthusiastically invited a batch of skeptical pastor friends to check out this new thing we'd cooked up. We started the evening with a few get-acquainted activities with about 25 people of mixed ages.

We had planned a live interview with Craig DeMartino, the survivor of a 100-foot mountain climbing fall. He was a living miracle, and he had a remarkable story to tell. His interview began…just as an ear-piercing alarm filled the air. Everyone cringed. None of us could figure out how to shut off the alarm system, which was just doing its job of announcing after-hours intruders. Thom and Craig shouted above the din, trying to share how the right attitude gets us through hard times. Then, finally, someone disarmed the alarm. Ahhh.

Then it was time for our creative prayer station experience in which individuals would ponder and pray as they connected with God. And then…the blasted alarm went off *again!* After a few more unbearable minutes, we figured out how to shut it off.

The group left, gracious and kind. Most never returned. It was terrible!

We drove home, and I (Joani) was in tears. We'd worked so hard. We'd invested hours and hours of thought and preparation. Why would God allow our first big night to be such a disaster?

The next morning, God revealed something even bigger to us: It wasn't about us. It wasn't about a perfectly planned performance. It was about *God.* And God wants us to give thanks in *all* circumstances. Remember?

Okay. Got it.

So that's how we began the planting of Lifetree Café. And God has been growing it ever since.

A NUDGE?

While we were first experimenting with Lifetree Café, we read this in The New York Times:

Religion and politics [...] are, of course, fundamentally different.

Politics is, by definition, a public activity. Though religion contains large public components, it is at core a personal affair. It is the relationship we have with ourselves or, as the British philosopher Alfred North Whitehead said, "What the individual does with his solitariness." There lies the problem: how to talk about the private nature of religion publicly. What is the solution? The answer, I think, lies in the sort of entrepreneurial spirit that has long defined America, including religious America. We need a Steve Jobs of religion. Someone (or ones) who can invent not a new religion but, rather, a new way of being religious. Like Mr. Jobs' creations, this new way would be straightforward and unencumbered and absolutely intuitive. Most important, it would be highly interactive. I imagine a religious space that celebrates doubt, encourages experimentation and allows one to utter the word God without embarrassment. A religious operating system for the Nones among us. And for all of us.[6]

After reading this, we couldn't help but wonder: Could this be the kind of "religious space" we're trying to create? Could this be another nudge from God to reach out in faith and experiment with such a place?

ANSWERING THE FOUR REASONS
Nobody Wants to Go to Church Anymore

After so often hearing the four cries of regular people, we decided to address them head-on as we shaped the national network of Lifetree Cafés. We wondered how Jesus would approach church today (feeling fairly certain he wouldn't be spending 20 or more hours a week preparing a 30-minute speech to deliver every Sunday morning).

How could we create a space that turns regular people's objections into affirmations?

When they say...	Imagine Jesus saying...	The church practices...
"I feel judged."	"You're welcome just as you are."	RADICAL HOSPITALITY
"I don't want to be lectured. You don't care what I think."	"Your thoughts are welcome; your doubts are welcome."	FEARLESS CONVERSATION
"Church people are a bunch of hypocrites."	"We're all in this together."	GENUINE HUMILITY
"Your God is irrelevant to my life."	"God is here, ready to connect with you in a fresh way."	DIVINE ANTICIPATION

In fact, these four cries form the basis of the Lifetree values that are posted and stated each week at every Lifetree Café:

"You're welcome just as you are.

Your thoughts are welcome; your doubts are welcome.

We're all in this together.

God is here, ready to connect with you in a fresh way."

These acts of love will make your church irresistible—because Jesus is irresistible.

THE CONVERSATION Café

As we experimented with this new way to "do church," we gradually developed a mixture of elements that created a place where real relationships—with God and others—can grow every time people gather. A place where all kinds of people—from believers to nonbelievers and everyone in between—gather to hear inspiring stories and engage in conversation on a different topic every week. It's led entirely by volunteers and revolves around a safe, welcoming environment where everyone gets to share thoughts and stories.

Lifetree Café became a very "non-churchy" place where people…

- enter a familiar coffeehouse-type setting (it's never big, it's familiar, and people don't worry about when to sit or stand).
- are greeted at the door with a smile.
- enjoy complimentary refreshments.
- are seated with up to three others at small, round tables.

We created a special time when people…

- have a one-hour experience at a convenient time of day or night (not necessarily Sunday morning).
- discuss topics relevant to their lives.
- experience inspiring, real-life stories on video and exclusive films.
- spend lots of time in guided conversation at their tables.
- experience a spiritual ah-ha that connects God to their everyday lives.
- explore the same topics as others across the country every week (both in person and online).
- can hang out "AfterWords" to continue the conversation and enjoy their growing friendships.

In all of this, we prayed that God would bring a breath of fresh air to the church through us.

We kept wondering *what if…*

What **IF…**

What if…churches offered a new way to experience God?

Research shows many people are looking for a new kind of spiritual expression. The Barna Group reports that half of Americans say a growing number of people they know "are tired of the usual type of church experience." And 64 percent say they are "completely open to carrying out and pursuing [their] faith in an environment or structure that differs from that of a typical church." Also, 75 percent say they sense that "God is motivating people to stay connected with Him, but in different ways and through different types of experiences than in the past."[7] These responses indicate the population's openness to the Lifetree Café approach.

What if…churches met the practical needs of the community?

We made sure that Lifetree Café offers help on a weekly basis for everyday life issues. People in every community are dealing with wayward children, aging parents, worry, addictions, obnoxious coworkers, stress, personal significance, financial struggles, and on and on. So we designed Lifetree Café to provide churches with an externally focused mission of meeting people where they're at with practical help.

What if…churches provided existing members with meaningful ministry opportunities?

Most churches report that only a minority of their people are actively involved in hands-on ministry. As we experimented with Lifetree Café, we wanted to offer a fresh, easy way for church members to serve. Even though most people want to feel needed, most churches struggle to find and keep volunteers for all their ministries. We know volunteers enjoy seeing real results firsthand. With Lifetree, they get to help regular people discover practical tools and tips for dealing with life's issues, experience God, and grow in their relationships with Christ and others.

What if…churches equipped existing members to "glow"?

Most church members today feel uncomfortable talking about their faith outside of church. We found that with Lifetree Café, people get meaningful, practical training to help them "let their lights shine" without repelling others. It gives members a safe, comfortable venue to share their personal faith stories naturally every week.

What if…churches closed the "back door"?

Church leaders know that newcomers entering the front door don't represent the whole picture. Those who eventually decide to slip out the back door and wander away can significantly dampen congregational growth. Some leave because of hurt feelings. Some leave because they're not actively involved. Some leave because they're burned out. Some leave because the existing ministry offerings don't connect with them. Some leave because the routine becomes too familiar and they feel spiritually stuck. As reported in the book *Reveal*, research in several notable churches showed that active, long-time, spiritually mature members were among those most likely to report they are considering leaving the church.[8] Lifetree Café offers those who are tempted to leave church a fresh way to grow spiritually—and even help others grow.

What if…churches provided an easy way for existing members to invite their neighbors?

Many people fear inviting their nonchurched friends to church. But they feel perfectly comfortable inviting friends to the local Starbucks for coffee and conversation. Similarly, they find it natural to invite friends to Lifetree for coffee, conversation, and an engaging hour focused on a topic their friends may find genuinely interesting.

What if…churches laid the foundation to plant a new church?

Some results of our Lifetree experiment thoroughly surprised us. We found that establishing a Lifetree Café in new areas can attract a following that may eventually provide the nucleus for a new church congregation. While Lifetree Café isn't necessarily viewed as a church, it provides the opportunity to meet people who may eventually show interest in supporting a new congregation.

What if…churches grew with a scalable model?

We found that the Lifetree Café framework offers a path to grow without relying on finite resources such as unusually gifted orators or musicians. As demand increases for each café, more sessions can be easily added. And since Lifetree uses volunteer staff, many additional people can be equipped to lead additional sessions. Some churches have even added additional Lifetree Café locations as they've grown.

What if…churches grew with a sustainable model?

One thing we know for sure: A church based on personalities is extremely limited in its potential, and eventually those central "celebrities" will go away. We made sure that Lifetree Café doesn't focus on personalities who can move away, get ill, retire, or fall into temptation. Our experiment works because it's staffed with a flow of eager volunteers who can sustain an ongoing ministry. This volunteer advantage is similar to other volunteer-led community organizations such as service clubs, scouts, and hobby groups.

What if...churches achieved visibility in the community?

When churches sponsor a Lifetree Café, they get a real chance to demonstrate outwardly focused love and service to their community. The practical help for life issues along with periodic service projects provides a regular—and newsworthy—gift to the community. We've found local news agencies around the country to be very eager to write about the subjects and events going on every week at Lifetree Café.

What if...churches became part of a local and national conversation?

Relationships happen on a very local level. But there's something special about being part of something bigger than yourself. Part of our experiment with Lifetree Café (and LifetreeCafé.com) includes creating a national conversation about the compelling topics of our day in a Christ-centered context. What you hear about in the news, what people are talking about at work and school, and what people are talking about online is what people talk about at Lifetree Café. Each week Lifetree Cafés from coast to coast focus on the same topic, simultaneously helping everyone see the presence, love, and action of the living God.

What if...church wasn't a bait and switch?

Church leaders often ask, "How will Lifetree Café visitors get connected to my church?" We always return them to Lifetree Café's ultimate purpose: to help people grow in relationship with the Lord. As that goal is accomplished, leaders of a church-sponsored Lifetree Café should hear, "Well done, my good and faithful servants." Lifetree Café participants take different avenues to grow in their relationships with the Lord. We relearned something we already knew: Jesus is "the way," but everyone walks a unique path to find him.

Lifetree Café is carefully designed to be welcoming to believers *and* not-yet believers, to the churched *and* unchurched.

Who Did We Design This New **EXPERIMENT FOR?**

The unchurched.

Lifetree Café was created for people who are not attracted to churches. While those of us in the church may believe we offer good on-ramps for everyone, "this is not the word on the street," according to author Doug Pollock in his book *God Space*. "For many who grew up outside the walls of the church, going to church is a scary proposition," he writes.[9]

We wanted to offer the unchurched a safe, small, conversational environment in a café-like setting. They hunger for God, but not in the package typically offered on Sunday morning.

UN CHURCH ED = MORE THAN **30**%

- More than 1 in 3 adults are unchurched.

- 125 million Americans are unchurched.
- The percent of people who say they "never" attend church has risen steadily over the last 30 years as people shift from infrequent attendance to nonattendance.
- *Unchurched* means they haven't attended a religious service of any type during the past year.[10]

The dechurched.

There are many people in every community who used to be active in the church. Different circumstances led them away from the church. Though they're not likely to return to what they fled, they typically value the fellowship of believers and spiritually curious people. Mary, a 60-ish pastor's daughter, said, "At church, I've heard it all. And I've seen it all. I moved on. I come to Lifetree because it gives me what I need—reminders of God's love from ordinary people living real lives."

The PIBOs.

These are church attendees who are Present In Body Only. They may be counted as members of a church's flock, but their hearts, minds, and souls are not engaged by what's happening at church. They're among the legion of church attendees who never experience God at church. They're just not into the sermons and sing-alongs. Many PIBOs find Lifetree Café experiences compelling because they're actively engaged in a different kind of personal relevancy.

A **REWARDING** Experiment

It's been several years since we started our Lifetree Café experiment, and it continues to be a work in progress. As of this writing, we have hundreds of Lifetree Cafés located in the U.S. and Canada, as well as a handful in other countries. It's been utterly amazing to see God work every single week in miraculous, unexpected ways. And we still feel as if we're barely getting started.

The next few chapters will focus on four powerful, practical tools for drawing people back to *your* church. We call them 4 ACTS OF LOVE. The Lifetree experiment has yielded countless stories of how they're making a real, life-changing difference in the lives of thousands of people around the country, so we'll use lots of Lifetree Café examples to help shed light on how they really work. But rest assured that *these examples, as well as the 4 ACTS OF LOVE, apply to any church that's serious about reaching the unchurched and dechurched.*

We hope church leaders and laypeople alike will understand the significance of these 4 ACTS OF LOVE and how they can truly transform your church into something everyone will run to...not away from.

Endnotes

1. Lee J. Colan, *Orchestrating Attitude* (Dallas, TX: CornerStone Leadership Institute, 2005), 43.

2. Wally Armstrong, *Practicing the Presence of Jesus* (Minneapolis, MN: Summerside Press, 2012), 30.

3. Ibid., 40.

4. Ibid., 42.

5. Jim Cymbala, *Fresh Wind, Fresh Fire* (Grand Rapids, MI: Zondervan, 2003), 30.

6. Eric Weiner, "Americans: Undecided About God?" *New York Times,* December 11, 2011, http://www.nytimes.com/2011/12/11/opinion/sunday/americans-and-god.html.

7. The Barna Group, "Americans Are Exploring New Ways of Experiencing God," June 8, 2009, http://www.barna.org/barna-update/article/12-faithspirituality/270-americans-are-exploring-new-ways-of-experiencing-god.html.

8. Greg L. Hawkins, Cally Parkinson, and Eric Arnson, *Reveal* (Barrington, IL: Willow Creek Resources, 2007), 53.

9. Doug Pollock, *God Space* (Loveland, CO: Group Publishing, 2009), 12.

10. Warren Bird, "More than 100 Million Unchurched in the United States?" *Learnings* (blog), Leadership Network, September 19, 2012, http://leadnet.org/blog/post/more_than_100_million_unchurched_in_the_united_states.

THE 4 ACTS OF LOVE

LOVE IS SOMETHING TO BE EXPERIENCED. You do it. It's an action.

> The Gobi desert in Mongolia is a dry, desolate, barren place. When we visited there a few years ago, we witnessed a miracle.

We were moving our stuff into our circular yurt (or "ger," as they're called there) and heard a ruckus from the locals. We ran outside to see what was happening. Apparently this lodge was located along a riverbed, but it had been dry for years. Now a spring of water was drizzling from a rock formation encircling the lodge area. We watched as the thread of water began to form a narrow stream and then an ever-widening river. The children had never seen water in that spot before. To the villagers, it was nothing short of a miracle.

It reminded us of this Scripture passage: "Look, a righteous king is coming! And honest princes will rule under him. Each one will be like a shelter from the wind and a refuge from the storm, like streams of water in the desert and the shadow of a great rock in a parched land. Then everyone who has eyes will be able to see the truth, and everyone who has ears will be able to hear it" (Isaiah 32:1-3).

Water in the desert! In that little Mongolian village we saw true joy and exuberance in people experiencing a life-giving marvel. It was real and tangible and yet utterly indescribable.

That's what love does.

Love is something to be experienced. You don't study it, nitpick it, blame it, or just talk or sing about it. You do it. It's an action.

And love dries up when it is not connected to the Source.

> **FOR LOVE COMES FROM GOD.** Everyone who loves has been born of God and knows God.
> — 1 John 4:7

Some say you can love without God, but we don't think so. You can't have power without a generator. We humans just aren't capable of being our own self-sustaining power source.

Sin happens when self is the source. Self-sourced marriages break up; self-sourced individuals experience constant conflict; and self-sourced lives lead to fighting, greed, secrets, lies, hurt, emptiness, fleeting relationships, and abuse of food, sex, drugs, and money. Too many marriages end with at least one partner saying, "I'm leaving because I'm just not happy anymore."

Like trying to conjure water out of rocks in the desert, without God we're left high and dry.

Being plugged into the Source means being fully charged and engaged, being a vessel for water to flow through. We can't just *go* to church, we must *be* the church. Our world will change when we stop thinking of church as something we attend and participate in and begin to think of it as people. William Paul Young, author of *The Shack*, says, "You can't go to something that you already are."[1]

Mission Arlington church in Arlington, Texas knows what it means to be the church. Led by Miss Tillie Burgin, Mission Arlington takes its tagline seriously: "Taking Church to the People." The church family serves the local community daily with health care ministries, counseling services, spiritual support, and more. Mission Arlington understands that *church* means so much more than sitting in a Sunday service—*church* is being the hands and feet of Jesus.

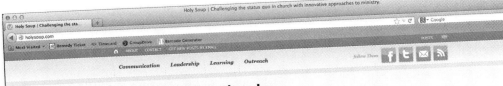

Thriving Among the Dying Churches

Last Sunday we drove past numerous half-empty church parking lots. Finally, we found our way to a thriving church that's bucking the trend—and breaking the rules.

Chances are you've never heard of the "lead pastor" (actually, they don't like titles here) who oversees one of the largest churches in America. More than 5,000 people gather each week in multiple locations throughout the area.

But this is no showy "multi-site" megachurch featuring some silver-tongued orator on a big screen. There's no professional praise band. No pipe organ. No fancy building.

This is no new church plant. It's been around for 27 years. And, unlike the majority of churches in America, it continues to grow.

Its leader is no twenty-something hipster. She (yes, *she*) is 76-year-old Tillie Burgin, a white-haired, soft-spoken Texan whom the locals call Miss Tillie. She leads Mission Arlington in the sprawling urban area between Dallas and Fort Worth.

We slipped inside Mission Arlington to film this story for our upcoming documentary on the state of the church in America. Many of our other stories depict the decline of the church. But this story illustrates several characteristics that renewed our hope for the future of the church.

Unlike so many other contemporary churches that tout the term "missional," this ministry consistently acts it out. Using the tagline

"Taking Church to the People," Mission Arlington directly serves hundreds of people every day of the week with spiritual, physical, and emotional support. It brings food, clothing, furniture, and medical care to all who need it.

And all are welcome. Miss Tillie likes to stress a particular word from John 3:16—"whosoever." And she doesn't wait for the whosoevers to come to her. She has empowered thousands of volunteers to take the church to the people.

Mission Arlington has formed 329 mini-congregations that meet weekly in houses, apartment complexes, mobile home parks, community centers, and playgrounds. When they fill the available space, they form a new little congregation at a different location. Volunteer ministers lead these small groups through simple Bible explorations for adults, youth, and children. If someone brings a guitar, they may sing a few songs.

And where's Miss Tillie? She's not preaching. She's not in the spotlight. She's back at the headquarters praying and encouraging more volunteers to go out to serve in the name of Christ. And her genuine humility is absolutely contagious.

But make no mistake. She gives all the credit to God. As we said goodbye Sunday afternoon, she cautioned us to get this story straight: "This is about what Jesus is doing here."

HolySoup.com

67

With God as the source, we've found the 4 ACTS OF LOVE to be powerful, authentic, life-changing ways for churched people to share God's love with the unchurched, the dechurched, and each other!

The 4 ACTS OF LOVE are, in essence and in practice, *how* to grow faith as a relationship.

Before we dive into each of the 4 ACTS OF LOVE, let's do a quick review of what they are and how they relate to the most common reasons people don't want to go to church anymore:

When they say...	Imagine Jesus saying...	The church practices...
"I feel judged."	"You're welcome just as you are."	RADICAL HOSPITALITY
"I don't want to be lectured. You don't care what I think."	"Your thoughts are welcome; your doubts are welcome."	FEARLESS CONVERSATION
"Church people are a bunch of hypocrites."	"We're all in this together."	GENUINE HUMILITY
"Your God is irrelevant to my life."	"God is here, ready to connect with you in a fresh way."	DIVINE ANTICIPATION

These 4 ACTS OF LOVE—radical hospitality, fearless conversation, genuine humility, and divine anticipation—will make your church irresistible because *Jesus* is irresistible. They really work, and we can honestly say we've witnessed the water flow in the desert countless times, week after week, for the last few years.

Everything we've learned from Lifetree Café is transferable to any church. Churches today are training Christians to share their faith, but it's like teaching swimming lessons without ever letting people get in the pool. Lifetree Café has been our swimming pool, and now the 4 ACTS OF LOVE can be yours.

Of course, your church doesn't have to open a Lifetree Café to put this kind of love into practice. Here's what we know from our experience with thousands of people during the last three or four years: When the four cries (why nobody wants to go to church anymore) meet these four Jesus-centered values, God's Spirit can't help but gush forth in miraculous ways.

The Church That
WOULDN'T BURN

> While on tour there, we walked past a decrepit, crumbling Anglican church.

Samarai Island was once a thriving village in the territory of Papua New Guinea. While on tour there, we walked past a decrepit, crumbling Anglican church. We learned that during World War II enemy forces burned the entire village with one exception: the church. Soldiers torched the building multiple times, but it would not burn. So it still stands today—a sad, decaying ruin of its former self. The timbers are rotting and the roof is nearly gone. Yet the legend of it standing through the fire lives on. Is this a parable for the church today? The church has miraculously avoided destruction in the past, but today it appears to be falling apart.

God will not give up on the church. For centuries, in spite of our shortcomings, Jesus' church continues. Jesus said, "Upon this rock I will build my church, and all the powers of hell will not conquer it" (Matthew 16:18). We don't believe the church will disappear into oblivion. But we know that we can't look in the mirror and walk away. Now is the time to take a deep breath and prepare to make some remarkable changes that will undoubtedly manifest some remarkable results.

Read on to see how every church can demonstrate 4 ACTS OF LOVE that will make it irresistible.

Endnotes

1. William Paul Young, "Spiritual but Not Religious,"
   Lifetree Café interview, Group Publishing,
   September 30, 2012.

2. Steve Hewitt, "Why is the church in America dying?
   Part 2," *Christian Computing Magazine*,
   August 2012, 5.

5

ACT OF LOVE #1
RADICAL HOSPITALITY

Sometimes you can't script a better story than the **ONES WRITTEN BY REAL LIFE.**

The week's topic at Lifetree Café was "Temptation: Why Good Men Go Bad." The hour promised an exclusive interview with Ted Haggard, the megachurch pastor who stayed with his wife and started a new church after his sizzling sex scandal with a male prostitute.

Not your everyday church topic.

Craig, Lifetree's national director, received this message on his phone: "Don't believe Haggard or give him the time of day!" said the voice claiming to be Mike Jones. Mike Jones? *The* Mike Jones? The male prostitute caught in the middle of the scandal?

Craig called Mike back to explain that Ted wasn't actually going to appear in person; his filmed interview would be discussed at that evening's Lifetree Café. Craig graciously invited Mike to come and participate in the discussion that night, which would take place about an hour's drive from Mike's home (RADICAL HOSPITALITY).

Even though Craig thought it unlikely that Mike would actually show up, Craig encouraged Mike to represent his side of the story.

Unknown to the other participants, Mike arrived and joined in the conversation at his table. After the first video segment, Mike raised his hand, faced the entire group, and declared, "I am the Mike Jones in the video."

Imagine their shock as the people at his table realized they'd been talking to the male prostitute featured in the story! But in true Lifetree fashion, they continued to welcome him into the conversation with openness and love (RADICAL HOSPITALITY).

The evening unfolded. They tackled the issue of temptation and grappled with Jesus' words from the Lord's Prayer, "Lead us not into temptation." The hour included Scripture, prayer, and a lively, honest discussion.

Toward the end of the evening, a man approached Mike and asked, "How did everything that happened to you change your view of God and the church?" Some of us were holding our breath, certain that the man would bombard Mike with a Scripture tirade. But no. They had a respectful conversation about struggling with the church while embracing God's love (RADICAL HOSPITALITY).

Expecting hostility in a setting known for its Christian values, Mike had encountered warmth instead. He stayed for almost an hour after the program talking with others. He appreciated the chance to be known and expressed his wish that a Lifetree Café existed near his home.

What's So Compelling About
RADICAL HOSPITALITY?

People like Mike have preconceived ideas about Christians. They expect us to be judgmental. So when they experience RADICAL HOSPITALITY, they're disarmed.

People who demonstrate this ACT OF LOVE are open to loving others without judging or looking down on them. They look past invisible differences (beliefs, attitudes, values, lifestyles) and visible differences (clothing, skin color, age, gender, economic status). RADICAL HOSPITALITY really does welcome people just as they are.

Barbara Huisman, pastor of Cana, speaks of the razor-thin edge between us all that makes each one of us the "least, lost, and lonely." In truth, we *all* need RADICAL HOSPITALITY.

Barbara's ministry welcomes the homeless who walk through her doors as warmly as those who drive up in their BMWs. It embraces people who struggle with lives full of poor choices and hardships as well as those who serve on various church staffs in town. Barbara and her people demonstrate a RADICAL HOSPITALITY that's magnetic. It's a powerful Jesus-style love that shines in the community.

When Jesus said, "You will be treated as you treat others," he was referring to the cyclical nature of human behavior. When the culture judges the church, we judge right back. And we want the culture to know it's misjudging us—we're not who they think we are. Likewise, people outside the church think the church is misjudging them, because *they're* not who *we* think they are. Only when walls come down through relationships do both sides have a chance of coming together.

> **DO NOT JUDGE OTHERS, AND YOU WILL NOT BE JUDGED.** For you will be treated as you treat others.
>
> — Matthew 7:1-2

Jesus-Style
RADICAL HOSPITALITY

In essence, Jesus says, "You're welcome just as you are." Throughout his ministry, Jesus embraced despised prostitutes, cheating tax collectors, smelly fishermen, and all manner of sinners. He reached out and touched the blind, the lame, even the "untouchables"—the lepers. Jesus opened his arms and welcomed others in such a radical way that the churchy types got pretty ticked! We humans would rather people clean up their acts *before* we connect with them. Thankfully, God doesn't think like that.

The New Testament is packed with unforgettable stories of Jesus' RADICAL HOSPITALITY. We love the story of Jesus' first encounter with Zacchaeus, a notorious cheat. It so vividly shows how religious people respond when Jesus reaches out to someone they don't think deserves it.

73

Jesus noticed Zacchaeus, called Zacchaeus to him, and invited himself over for dinner. The resulting change in Zacchaeus was miraculous. And the reaction of the religious people was, well, disturbing.

> "So we have stopped evaluating others from a human point of view. At one time we thought of Christ merely from a human point of view. How differently we know him now! This means that **ANYONE WHO BELONGS TO CHRIST HAS BECOME A NEW PERSON. THE OLD LIFE IS GONE; A NEW LIFE HAS BEGUN!**"
>
> — 2 Corinthians 5:16-17

cceptance
Without Endorsement
A Travel Parable From Mongolia

The people of Mongolia know about RADICAL HOSPITALITY. Hundreds of miles separate settlements. People open their homes and offer something to eat and drink to weary travelers. Hospitality is a big deal in this vast, sprawling landscape.

We experienced Mongolia's warmth and hospitality in some unforgettable ways. Friendly Mongolians welcomed us into their homes: round, felt, collapsible gers made for their nomadic lifestyle. Our hosts filled a communal bowl with fermented mare's milk and passed it from one person to the next. Imagine putting your lips to the pungent milk—a taste that resembles a concoction of sour milk, warm beer, and pickle juice.

We'll never forget ceremoniously passing the bowl from one guest to the next. Both of us had read in the travel books: "Just touch your lips to the bowl; don't drink the milk." Unfortunately, we hadn't instructed our son, Matt, on that little detail. Before we had a chance to signal to Matt, we saw him chugging the milk. Blech! *You're going to be so, so sick*, we thought. Sure enough, that night Matt was the sickest we'd ever seen him.

We love to share this story when we explain the difference between acceptance and endorsement. Traveling to Mongolia—or any other foreign culture—introduces us to people whose lifestyles, actions, looks, and belief systems are radically different from our own. We can kindly accept those differences (touch our lips to the mare's milk), but we don't have to endorse them (guzzle it down).

ACT OF LOVE #1 **RADICAL HOSPITALITY**

DON'T FORGET TO SHOW HOSPITALITY TO STRANGERS, for some who have done this have entertained angels without realizing it!

— Hebrews 13:2

How to Recognize
RADICAL HOSPITALITY

RADICAL HOSPITALITY is…

- **authentically welcoming others and being glad to be with them.**
  It's a genuine part of someone's personality—something that flows naturally. For example, when a woman who believed in the power of horoscopes and crystals attended Lifetree Café, we loved the opportunity to include her and share in conversation. Instead of being repulsed by someone with a different point of view, we relished the time with her so she could see Christians in a loving, nonjudgmental light, a light that opened the door to friendship and deeper conversations about Jesus.

- **caring curiosity.** You've heard the saying, "To be *interesting*, you need to be *interested*." When you notice someone and are really interested in connecting, that person knows it. Your conversation revolves around the other person rather than you. Your conversation isn't awkward or pushy. It's unscripted love.

- **being a friend even though it's not your "job."** Too many churches have systematized hospitality by creating jobs for greeters and helpful parking lot attendants. It's their task to make a good first impression so visitors will feel good about the church. That's all great. But here's the surprise: The most important 10 minutes at church happen *after* church services when it's nobody's "official duty" to be friendly, according to Gary L. McIntosh and Charles Arn in their book *What Every Pastor Should Know.*[2]

People know whether someone's sincerely interested in them. This is precisely why we let friends at Lifetree Café know they can hang around as long as they like. And they do—often for an hour after the program has officially ended. It's during this "AfterWords" period (we even gave the time a name because we know it's so important) that people linger, follow up on conversations sparked earlier, and talk about what's important to them.

I (Joani) encountered a great example of RADICAL HOSPITALITY on one of my "Jeanne Joani Journeys." Jeanne and I have been friends for more than 35 years, and every so often we like to meet in interesting places for a weekend and invest in our friendship. On one of those trips, Jeanne and I scoured the local listings and Internet for a church to visit on Sunday. Here's what transpired:

We were greeted by a smiling woman who said, "I don't think I've met you before." We explained that we were visiting the area on one of our favorite things to do together as friends—our "JJJs" (Jeanne Joani Journeys). She comfortably engaged in small talk with us and then pointed us toward the fellowship room for coffee and treats. With a glimmer in her eye, she said, "You can take your coffee into the sanctuary. We weren't always able to do that, but we changed the rules so we can now!" With a smile and a nod, she passed us onto another woman near the fellowship room door who welcomed us and made sure we were taken care of.

Once in the sanctuary, another woman turned around, leaned over the pew, and greeted us. She wasn't "on duty." She was a natural part of a radically hospitable church. We felt very welcome in this church.

- **accepting, no matter what**. People's age, gender, looks, dress, economic status—and whatever else makes them unique—don't make a difference. They're all God's children, and they see Jesus in action through you. Practically, this may mean doing the opposite of what your gut tells you to do. When someone looks odd, smells funny, or is angry or disagreeable, our natural response is to move away, not toward. "Accepting, no matter what" means asking the Holy Spirit to take over and prompt us to love others with an unconditional love that can only come from God.

One of our ministry friends laments his church's view of its youth ministry. When teenagers who smoke, use drugs, are troubled, at-risk, or messed up—teenagers who may need Jesus' love the most—want to attend youth group, church leaders prefer them to be relegated to a separate group. They don't like the idea of their kids mingling with them. "Accepting, no matter what" does not come naturally to the powers that be. In fact, many churches that insist on having youth ministries really use them as a veiled attempt to keep their good, churched kids away from the riffraff. How different and radical is a Jesus-style approach!

- **profoundly relational.** The Bible commonly uses relational phrases to describe the connection between God and us. Some examples: parent/child, father/son, father/daughter, bride/groom, vine/branch, hen/chick, sheep/shepherd. We talk about a relationship with God, but have we acted as if it is a *real* relationship?

We wondered how human relationships actually play into our relationship with God, especially after a Lifetree Café episode called "Spiritual but Not Religious." I (Joani) sat with one woman who used to go to church and another who'd never gone to church. The host posed the question, "Who has been part of your spiritual journey?" The former churchgoer told of attending church with her grandmother, a Christian. The other woman, who considered herself spiritual but not religious, paused. She couldn't think of a single person. Finally she said, "Oh yeah, the Dalai Lama." She couldn't name one person who walked with her on her spiritual journey other than a famous person she'd only read about! Clearly, she didn't have that kind of personal relationship in her life.

We can't underestimate God's powerful plan: *We* are the ones entrusted to embody Jesus and show people the love of God. To *live* that love, not merely study it. To *do* love, not just listen to a pastor talk about it.

For people to realize God is real and not just a concept, we need to put his love into action through relationships with those in our circles of influence—our family, friends, coworkers, and schoolmates.

- **something that takes time.** RADICAL HOSPITALITY is not just about making a great first impression. It's more than remembering and knowing people's names. It is that—but it's so much more. It takes time to get to know people, to really know them. And this is a rare, priceless, delicate gift. For when someone is really known and loved

78

over time through the roller coaster of life, he or she glimpses God's unconditional love. We need to look far beyond quick "decisions for Christ" and head-counting altar calls. Deep relationships marinate over time. We can't be in a hurry when it comes to love.

- **unnerving, surprising, and messy.** We live in a culture of celebrity, fame, Facebook, Twitter, and layer upon layer of façade. When you exude RADICAL HOSPITALITY, some people might not initially believe it's genuine because that kind of caring is so rare. It's a glimpse of God's unconditional love.

Loving unconditionally means being willing to love and give without expecting anything in return. Yes, we might be taken advantage of. Yes, we might not get more money in the offering plate. Yes, we might get hurt. When we imagine how bad it can get, we only need to look to the Cross. God's sacrifice of his Son was the ultimate act of unconditional love. And we are called to love as Jesus does, with God's same miraculous power. We just have to be willing vessels for this kind of love.

> "Above all, **CLOTHE YOURSELVES WITH LOVE, WHICH BINDS US ALL TOGETHER IN PERFECT HARMONY.** And whatever you do or say, **DO IT AS A REPRESENTATIVE OF THE LORD JESUS,** giving thanks through him to God the Father."
>
> — Colossians 3:14, 17

> "I wanted to counter the consumer attitude that uses the Bible as a way to gather religious data by which we can be our own gods, and then replace it with an attitude primed to listen to and obey God, to take us out of our preoccupations with ourselves into the spacious freedom in which God is working the world's salvation.[3]
>
> — Eugene Peterson, *Eat This Book*

RADICAL HOSPITALITY is <u>not</u>…

- **greeters at the door.** Well-meaning churches think if we plant bodies at the church doorways, we have accomplished our mission of hospitality. Too often, official greeters are completing a task they've been assigned—to smile and shake hands. There's nothing sincere or relational about that checklist duty.

- **meet-and-greet time in the service.** Some churches ask people to greet each other at the start of the worship service. Some call it the passing of the peace. If you're near and dear to those around you, it can be sort of fun and semi-fulfilling. But if you're surrounded by strangers, it can be awkward and stiff. The hope that this portion of the service demonstrates warmth and friendliness may be more the pastor's wish than reality. No relationships are formed during these fruitless 15 seconds.

- **coffee and doughnuts or an espresso bar.** A great idea and always a nice treat! But the presence of goodies in itself doesn't translate into RADICAL HOSPITALITY. Refreshments must be accompanied by friendly people. Too often church coffee time devolves into cliques, and new people are (often unintentionally) excluded from the circles of conversation. Installing a coffee bar is only half a step in the right direction.

- **parking lot attendants.** As incredible as it seems that churches have so much traffic they need to enlist people to wave safety flags, don't be fooled. Traffic cops are there to enforce rules, not direct people toward RADICAL HOSPITALITY.

- **a come-to-our-deal event.** Churches have outdone themselves in finding creative ways to invite new people, advertising everything from comedy shows to "Come to our church and win a free car!" As outgoing and robust as these outreach efforts may be, they're still inviting people to *our* thing, which communicates that it's about *us*. Outreach events are fun, but they don't necessarily result in changed lives or lasting relationships—even if an altar call or gospel presentation is tacked on. We may like to count noses, but RADICAL HOSPITALITY is much harder because it requires genuine investment in the lives of others.

- **a bait and switch.** People not connected with the Lord have built-in radar to detect this. Those who don't see value in church are doubly suspicious of invitations or relationships that seem inauthentic. While on a college campus, our daughter-in-law was invited to coffee by a well-meaning campus minister. (That *could* be a good thing.) It didn't take long for her to realize he wasn't really interested in her as a person; he was interested in "gaining a notch in his spiritual belt," spouting Bible verses and frowning on her naïveté about the Bible. It left a sour taste in her mouth—and she's a believer! It was the last time she attended that campus ministry's meetings.

Beware: People in authentic relationships are in them for the long haul. And they're in them for the right reasons. The campus minister didn't live up to the common expectation of what it means to meet a friend for coffee. When you want to build a relationship, do what a real friend would do.

- **guestbook signing.** Okay, we admit it: We always invite visitors to our home to sign our personal guestbook. We think of it as getting celebrities' autographs. And I (Joani) like to say, "The only thing we ask of you is to sign the guestbook. After that, you don't have to do anything else. Just relax and have a good time." But churches that rely on guestbooks to capture guests may not be capturing much of anything.

- **awarding prize points for bringing visitors.** Far too many churches have used the bribe technique to get us to invite friends to church. How would you feel if you discovered you were invited to something so that the person who invited you could get a prize? Did your friend really want to be with you and care about your connection with Jesus—or were you just used so he or she could win a prize?

- **a strict list of "approved" stuff.** Churches are notorious for their lists of do's and don'ts concerning food, music, dress, looks, jewelry—whatever. All of these rules exclude others and are just one more sign that we're judgmental and have our priorities wrong. We have a friend whose daughter was reprimanded for showing up at her on-campus Bible study in running pants. Really?

- **scripted.** RADICAL HOSPITALITY doesn't make use of a rehearsed script outlining four spiritual laws or the sinner's prayer or clichés. Rather, it entails genuine conversations in which we rely on the Holy Spirit and trust God to act through us as we interact with others.

In our experiment with Lifetree Café, we've learned to depend on these unscripted conversations. Candace told us about her experience after one episode called "The Bible: Real? Relevant? Reliable?" It attracted Christians and non-Christians alike. One group of four skeptical men nabbed Candace at the end of the hour and said, "Hey, you're a Christian. Come over here and answer some of our questions." *Gulp*. She wasn't an expert theologian or Bible scholar, but she prayed God would give her the right words to say. Armed with a Koran, the Book of Mormon, and a Bible, the men wanted to know more about the Bible, the Word of God. For the next hour, Candace trusted the Holy Spirit to speak through her. And God did! Those men still come back every week to grapple with their questions in that safe, relational setting where God shows up in a fresh way—through unscripted conversations like the one they had with Candace.

DO: Put first impressions of your church to the test. Arm an unrecognized person with a hidden video camera and have the person enter your church on a Sunday morning. Afterward, talk with your "secret shopper" about what happened; then show the video to your leaders. Celebrate what you find—or decide what needs to change—to help ensure that people always experience RADICAL HOSPITALITY when they enter your church.

The Lord **LOOKS AT THE HEART.** — 1 Samuel 16:7

Now that you have a better understanding of what RADICAL HOSPITALITY is, let's dive into some practical ways to make it work in your church.

Endnotes

1. Doug Pollock, *God Space* (Loveland, CO: Group Publishing, 2009), 31.

2. Gary L. McIntosh and Charles Arn, *What Every Pastor Should Know: 101 Indispensable Rules of Thumb for Leading Your Church* (Grand Rapids, MI: Baker Books, 2013), 35.

3. Eugene H. Peterson, *Eat This Book* (Grand Rapids, MI: Eerdmans Publishing, 2006), 176.

6 PRACTICAL WAYS TO LOVE WITH RADICAL HOSPITALITY

Let us continue to LOVE ONE ANOTHER, FOR LOVE COMES FROM GOD.

First John 4:7-8 says, "Dear friends, let us continue to love one another, for love comes from God. Anyone who loves is a child of God and knows God. But anyone who does not love does not know God, for God is love."

If we truly believed this, our churches would be very different. In fact, *your* church can be very different this week! And you don't have to reinvent everything you're doing. All it takes is a shift in focus and an understanding of what actually works.

This chapter offers you some proven, practical ways to make RADICAL HOSPITALITY work in your church ministry. We've seen firsthand how each of these things really, truly connects you with the dechurched, the unchurched, and, well, even the churched.

EMBRACE THE POWER of Environment

Most of us underestimate the power of our surroundings. Much of our work to ensure RADICAL HOSPITALITY is done before anyone says a word. People soak in their surroundings—and those surroundings create feelings.

83

Howard Schultz, chairman and CEO of Starbucks, says that when setting out to create an atmosphere for selling coffee, his team researched the vibe people longed for—a comfortable "third place," a place conducive to relationship building. Their research had nothing to do with the menu, prices, or where the coffee beans are grown.

"I see a deep sense of community," Schultz says about the Starbucks environment. "We've intended, from day one, to really kind of build a third place between home and work. And really, I think at a time in America where people are hungry for human connection, we're providing that."[1]

Church, take note. If we don't want to be seen as any of the places along the streetscape described in Chapter 2, we need to create environments for RADICAL HOSPITALITY. Some churches have gotten on the coffee shop bandwagon, building comfortable spaces for mingling. Now we need to allow that special place to be a physical center of real ministry, not just a cool place to hang out.

Famed Canadian philosopher Marshall McLuhan (the man who predicted the World Wide Web 30 years before it existed) is known for coining the phrase, "The medium is the message." He understood that the *way* we communicate is more important than the things we say. In the case of the church environment, we should never underestimate the significance of "territory." Neither hallowed halls of stained glass nor theater-style arenas nurture the intimacy personal relationships require.

We need to be shrewd in understanding how things actually work, especially when it comes to the atmosphere in which we hope faith will grow. Like it or not, the unchurched and the dechurched are never going to hear what we say if they're not comfortable with how we're saying it.

Take a look at the graphic below about the effectiveness of communication. The church needs to take this seriously.

7% CONTENT

38% SOUND

55% LOOK

Like getting the rocket's payload (content) into space, the rocket's boosters (sound and look) get it off the ground.

> Some churches have gotten on the coffee shop bandwagon, building comfortable spaces for mingling. Now we need to allow that special place to be a physical center of real ministry, not just a cool place to hang out.

35% NO COFFEE AREA

65% YES COFFEE AREA

[3]

Homey Hope for the Homeless

After helping the homeless through a special Lifetree Café outreach, Barb and Dennis Miller had an idea. They wondered if they could offer Lifetree episodes at a homeless shelter—going to the people, instead of asking them to come to us. They recruited volunteers among the homeless who frequented the shelter and turned a stark, well-worn area into a warm, inviting conversation café. The nurturing atmosphere gave the displaced a place of their own—somewhere they felt truly at home. You should have seen the wide eyes and heard the words of appreciation from the folks who frequent that space—and who now join in weekly topical conversations about their faith.

"We are a rural church in Canada. Two years ago, we began to feel that we should get rid of our pews that seat 500 people and replace them with round tables, chairs, and couches. We organized them in a circle, brought in toys for babies, tables for children to color on, food, drink…This decision was never about being trendy; it stemmed from an overwhelming sense that the Holy Spirit was leading and driving this feeling. And we did it. The sense of community instantly changed. Our thinking has been challenged in many ways as we've asked questions such as 'How do I sing standing around a table?' 'Should we stand?' 'Can I worship with a cup of coffee in my hand?' 'What about the carpet?' and 'Can I worship without looking at someone's back?' We had to model again and again that it was all right…"[4]

— L.L.

WHY NOBODY WANTS TO GO TO CHURCH ANYMORE

Understand the **POWER OF LANGUAGE**

Get rid of churchy jargon.

The primary problem with using Christian "code words" is that most unchurched people have no idea what we're talking about. The last thing we want is for our guests to feel like outsiders. If we're to find common ground and eliminate barriers to relationships, exclusive language has to go.

If you're not sure how to go about it, turn it into a game. Ask a group to brainstorm words or phrases that might be hard for someone outside your church to understand. This includes acronyms, abbreviations, nicknames, pet names, long words, and doctrinal terms. Then decide if those words or phrases need to remain in your vocabulary. (If they do, you might follow our church's example; we put definitions of liturgical words in the church newsletter or bulletin.) Anything that "regular people" wouldn't understand needs to disappear for good.

It's not called RADICAL hospitality for nothing.

Carefully choose which words will help you communicate. For example, we've found that people may be "guests" and "strangers" in the parking lot, but once they walk through the doors they're our "friends." A ministry that works with street kids, Dry Bones, trains its volunteers to call the homeless children "friends," too. Just the word *friend* steers your mindset in a caring, loving direction. Instead of viewing newcomers or homeless children as projects or targets, it helps us remember that, as people, we're "all in this together." (More about that in Chapter 10: Practical Ways to Love With GENUINE HUMILITY.)

Remember, it's not about sounding academic or profoundly knowledgeable. It's about doing your part to build a relationship.

Take Time for
"BEFRIENDING"

Years of experience have taught us the value of taking time to build relationships—even with those who have known each other for years. Discovering something new about another person never gets old. Both of us love pairing up with a coworker or new acquaintance to answer a question that reveals something we hadn't known about the other. After decades of immersing ourselves in children, youth, and adult ministry and studying group dynamics, training leaders, and leading Group, we can testify to the importance of befriending in building trust and rapport.

Be intentional. Relationships don't just happen. Just because people are meeting in the same location doesn't mean relationships are forming. They take deliberate thought and leadership.

Don't count on technology to do the work for you, either. Sociologist Sherry Turkle, author of *Alone Together*, worked in the forefront of technology before seeing the unintended consequences of the Internet, social media, and cell phone communication.

In this high-tech world we live in, communication is constantly available to us through Facebook, Twitter, LinkedIn, and more; so it's tempting to think we're more connected than ever, Turkle explains. "We expect more from technology and less from each other. [Technology is the] illusion of companionship without the demands of friendship," she writes.[5]

Make personal relationship building a priority every time people come together. Genuine, fully engaged, face-to-face time is what really counts. At Group, we build befriending moments into all our staff meetings and gatherings, and the positive consequences have been remarkable in building a caring, supportive environment.

Here are a few examples of what we call befriending questions:

- When you think of the word *vacation*, what comes to mind?
- Share a piece of good news you heard this week.
- What was your connection to animals when you were young?
- Briefly describe your dream home…and where it would be.
- What's something your mom said or did that you now find *yourself* saying or doing?
- When you were a child, how did you celebrate your birthday?

- If you had a free day—one with absolutely no obligations—what would you do with it?
- When you were little, what did you want to do when you grew up?
- Tell about a brush with greatness you've had. Someone you've sort of met or someone that someone you know knows.
- What kind of traveler are you?
- Would you rather watch *Dancing with the Stars* or actually dance on the show?

Remember Friends and Family **BRING FRIENDS AND FAMILY**

Churches hope that an advertisement on TV, the radio, a billboard, the Web, or in print will draw people to them. Those may be great marketing tools...for soda and car sales. But far and away the most powerful attractor to church is word of mouth—a friend inviting a friend.

If you want to demonstrate true RADICAL HOSPITALITY, chuck your marketing plans out the window. Seriously. Mass media is the opposite of personal. Faith grows through relationships, not clever slogans in drive-by ads. Instead of paying for fliers or commercials, encourage the friends and families in your church to invite *their* friends and families. But make sure what you're inviting them to is something more than a cliché of church.

Creative invitations work. Our friend Dave Hurlbutt bubbled over with enthusiasm as he told us about his neighbor. After years of building a wall between himself and the church, Dave's neighbor finally came to Lifetree Café. Dave said this of his neighbor:

"[He was] blown away by this relationship we have with God that he can see in people he's getting to know from Hope [Dave's church] and Lifetree. As a child, he was taught God is a mean judge just waiting to lower the boom. I cried tears of joy when he recognized that we have a God who talks to us, who is a friend. Praise God for this revelation! And hear this: He admitted that although he receives the emails about upcoming Lifetree episodes, he wouldn't have come if I hadn't invited him. Let that be a bold reminder to all of us of how important a personal touch is!"

Understand the
POWER OF NAMES

People of all ages love to hear others use, remember, or call their names (in a kind and loving way, of course). Instead of making excuses for not remembering names, find ways for you and your team to improve.

Help people learn each other's names. Wear name tags. Do mixers and icebreakers every time you get together. Play simple games that encourage people to use their names. Say a person's name every time you talk to him or her. It's affirming, and no one can get too much affirmation.

People marvel at our pastor's ability to remember names. It means so much to people. He's a far cry from the pastor of a church we used to attend. Every week after the worship service, that pastor would shake Thom's hand and say, "Good to see you, Thom." Then he'd shake Joani's hand and say, "Blessings to you." We shared plenty of laughs about Joani's new nickname: "Blessings to you."

> "I have **CALLED YOU BY NAME**; you are mine." — Isaiah 43:1

Get Better Acquainted Through
PERSONAL
STORYTELLING

Lyman Coleman, the "grandpappy" of relational ministry, taught us the importance of giving people nonthreatening ways to learn more about each other. The easiest way? Ask people to share something about themselves that can't be interpreted as right or wrong. It's their story—their personal history.

90

We use this storytelling technique with all ages. Children love telling about themselves. Adults do, too. We call this "Tell about a time..." Whatever the topic, we find ways to ask people to tell about their lives. The beauty of this technique is that people can choose to share at whatever level they find comfortable. It's like deciding what end of the pool you want to enter—the shallow or the deep end. It's up to you.

Here are some examples from actual Lifetree episodes:

- Share a story of a failure you've survived.
- Tell about either the worst job or best job you've ever had.
- When was a time in your life when someone would have described you as a "glass half-empty" sort of person?
- Tell about a time it felt as if your life was going up in flames.
- Tell about something from your childhood that's been tough to deal with.
- Tell about a time you struggled to forgive. What happened...and how do you feel about it now?

Set the **TONE**

If you want others to open up and be vulnerable, set the example. Too often we've seen insecure leaders use humor or cynicism or share inappropriate stuff that just makes everyone squirm. Church leaders are the model for others. If leaders are insecure, unsure, fearful, or unwilling to risk themselves, you can be sure the entire church, group, or class will reflect that.

When you ask other people to "tell about a time," you should go first. This helps people understand expectations and open up with their own stories. As you provide a living example of growing faith through relationships, people will follow.

Our friend Theresa Mazza told me (Joani) about a neighborhood party her family was invited to. It's a great metaphor for what happens when we invite people to church and the difference a leader can make in welcoming newcomers.

91

To begin with, the neighborhood friend did a kind thing: She invited her neighbors to a party. (Imagine how often we tell churchgoers to invite a friend to church...and then we stop there.)

Theresa's family felt a bit uncomfortable about agreeing to go because they didn't know anyone else at the party, but they felt they should go anyway. (Imagine deciding to attend church.)

Once they arrived, the experience spiraled downward. They didn't know a soul. And no one introduced them to anyone. (Imagine how hard it is for someone to make the effort to come to church and then be greeted by...no one.)

Everyone else seemed happy to chat in their existing circle of friends. (Imagine watching others at church chat with their friends.)

Theresa's family sat and ate in awkward silence while everyone else partied on. (Imagine awkwardly doing what you think is required, wondering how long this experience will last.)

Finally, after an hour or so, the host invited Theresa's family to join in a game. At last someone welcomed them, reached out, and included them. (Imagine how wonderful it can be when "the leader sets the tone.")

Theresa and I talked about RADICAL HOSPITALITY and the importance of being in tune with how others may be feeling and taking the lead in making them feel genuinely welcome. Churches—and, most important, individuals—need to look outside themselves to treat others as they would want to be treated.

> "When I am with those who are weak, I share their weakness, for I want to bring the weak to Christ. Yes, **I TRY TO FIND COMMON GROUND WITH EVERYONE, DOING EVERYTHING I CAN TO SAVE SOME.**"
>
> — 1 Corinthians 9:22

Eat **TOGETHER**

For years we've joked about church potlucks, Sunday morning coffee and doughnuts, teen pizza parties, and vacation Bible school snacks. But there's more power in eating together than we realize. A Gallup survey explored the link between friendship and faith, and the research revealed that church attendees who share meals together experience higher church satisfaction. Those who share meals together are three times more likely to say they're highly satisfied with their church.[6]

In their book *Many Tables*, Dennis E. Smith and Hal E. Taussig write, "In the New Testament, it is notable that Jesus is defined as a 'friend of tax collectors and sinners' precisely by his act of dining with them."[7] Pharisees and teachers of the law were often caught muttering, "This man welcomes sinners and eats with them" (Luke 15:2).

The authors call it "banquet friendship," which resulted when people left behind "the divisive social rankings of outer society and in effect [formed] a new society with new social rules."[8] Jesus rocked cultural barriers simply by eating with others.

In his book *The Friendship Factor*, Alan Loy McGinnis writes, "There is something almost sacramental about breaking bread with another and it is almost impossible to have dinner with an enemy and remain enemies."[9]

By sharing food, your church can break down social barriers to create common experiences that "form a new society." Bring on the potlucks, barbeques, snacks, and desserts. Try home dinner groups, dinner-and-a-movie nights, and coffee shop get-togethers. Have your meetings at restaurants. Capitalize on heightened interest in cooking shows and exotic foods. Enlist the "foodies" in your midst, who may include many young adults.

Those who share meals together are three times more likely to say they're highly satisfied with their church.

3x more likely to be satisfied

Don't Underestimate the
POWER OF A SMILE

Just smile! Offer others the gift of your smile. Not only does a smile convey warmth and the beginnings of RADICAL HOSPITALITY, it also makes *you* feel better. You've heard it said, "If you have the joy of the Lord, tell your face."

A study published in the journal *Psychological Science* "confirms the benefits of the warm gesture: When pedestrians on a busy street walked past a stranger who smiled at them, they felt more connected to others. Researchers note that even small acts of kindness can ward off feelings of isolation and ostracism, plus foster a sense of fraternity and compassion within the community—factors linked to the cultivation of long-term happiness."[10]

Be **PATIENT**

In an age of "instant everything," remember that RADICAL HOSPITALITY takes time. Be willing to invest in someone's life for the long haul. Embracing the maxim "You're welcome just as you are" means trusting God's timing, purposes, and processes. Just as it takes time for a tree to grow, for fine wine to age—for any masterpiece to be created—relationships developed through RADICAL HOSPITALITY take time.

The bottom line of RADICAL HOSPITALITY: Be a friend. Don't even think about what a *church* should do. Do what *friends* would do. It's the hospitable thing to do. And these days, it's the radical thing to do.

Endnotes

1. CBS News, "Starbucks CEO Howard Schultz is all abuzz," March 27, 2011, http://www.cbsnews.com/8301-3445_162-20047618/starbucks-ceo-howard-schultz-is-all-abuzz.html.

2. Philip Graves, quoted in Bruce Horovitz, "McDonald's revamps stores to look more upscale," USA Today, May 9, 2011, http://usatoday30.usatoday.com/money/industries/food/2011-05-06-mcdonalds-revamp_n.htm.

3. Group Publishing, "Does Your Church Have a Coffee Area?" Survey, May 2008.

4. Liz Lapsley, September 2, 2012 (8:53 p.m.), comment on Thom Schultz, "What Church Looks Like—in 10 Years," *Holy Soup* (blog), July 25, 2012, http://holysoup.com/2012/07/25/what-church-looks-like-in-10-years.

5. Sherry Turkle, *Alone Together* (New York, NY: Basic Books, 2011), xii, 1.

6. Group Publishing, *Friendship: Creating a Culture of Connectivity in Your Church* (Loveland, CO: Group Publishing, 2005), 11.

7. Dennis E. Smith and Hal E. Taussig, *Many Tables: The Eucharist in the New Testament and Liturgy Today* (Philadelphia, PA: Trinity Press International, 1990), 31.

8. Ibid., 34.

9. Alan Loy McGinnis, *The Friendship Factor* (Minneapolis, MN: Augsburg Fortress, 2004), 53.

10. *First for Women*, "The power of a single smile," October 1, 2012, 50.

7

When we trust the Holy Spirit, **GOD WILL TAKE CARE OF THE REST.**

It promised to be an hour of conversation and stories to feed the soul. But the program was advertised as "The Witch Next Door"—not exactly what you might expect in a venue designed to talk about faith.

The Lifetree Café space filled up with new faces; some claimed to be Wiccan, some pagan, some Jewish, some Christian, and some who claimed no faith at all. The hour began with nonthreatening befriending questions before launching into filmed interviews with a witch (a beautiful woman you'd probably never picture as such), a pagan couple who'd been disillusioned by the church, and a former Wiccan turned Christian. Each story gripped the group with its raw honesty and straightforwardness.

After the interviews, people engaged in respectful conversations. Toward the end of the hour, everyone received a handout listing the beliefs of Wiccans, pagans, and Christians. The host asked us to read the handout and then share at our tables which beliefs we held and why (FEARLESS CONVERSATION).

My (Joani's) partner happened to be Jewish, just another example of the wide diversity of beliefs represented at Lifetree Café. It offered me a danger-free and caring avenue for sharing my Christian faith with someone curious to know why I believe what I do. Everyone left surprised that dialogue among people with such different beliefs would be encouraged in a Christian environment (FEARLESS CONVERSATION). It was a great opportunity for believers to share our faith in a nonthreatening way.

The hour flew by. But that wasn't the end. God continued to surprise me. I returned to my desk later that day to find an email that read something like this: "That session really messed with my mind. I feel all tangled up now. I went home and dug out a Koran and a Bible. I don't know what I believe anymore."

Oh great, I thought. *That Lifetree hour totally bombed! How could that happen? Why did our time together hurt someone more than help?*

I prayed for God to give me the right words (FEARLESS CONVERSATION). I tapped out this email: "I'm sorry you're feeling confused. Please keep coming to Lifetree because it's a great place to untangle…"

I can't remember what else I wrote. All I know is that the idea of FEARLESS CONVERSATION felt really scary. Why would God let conversations about God backfire like that?

The next day, I got another email from the same person: "Thanks. I read my Bible. I know who really loves me and who I believe in. I've rededicated my life to Jesus."

Wow! God is more amazing and wonderful than we can ever imagine. He showed me that when we trust the Holy Spirit, he will take care of the rest. That's a promise!

> " I planted the seed in your hearts, and Apollos watered it, **BUT IT WAS GOD WHO MADE IT GROW.** " — 1 Corinthians 3:6

WHAT'S SO COMPELLING
About FEARLESS CONVERSATION?

Many non-churchgoers say, "You Christians just lecture me. You don't care what I think." So when they hear us tell them, "Your thoughts are welcome, and your doubts are welcome," they're genuinely stunned. It opens the door for God to work.

"Wait…what? You actually care about me and what I think? Hmm. Maybe I'll listen to what you have to say, since you've honored me by caring about me first."

In its simplest form, this ACT OF LOVE means we listen. To listen we allow two-way conversation. An honest, authentic, two-way dialogue is amazingly refreshing in a culture that craves conversation.

The church needs more FEARLESS CONVERSATIONS. An event following one Lifetree Café episode explains why: Ruth, a lovely and articulate older woman, spoke to the host following the hour-long program, saying, "I love coming to Lifetree because I can ask questions here. When I was 10 years old, I got kicked out of Sunday school because I asked too many questions. And I haven't been back to church since." Her story may alarm you, but it's only one of hundreds like it we've heard over the years.

Another ah-ha moment came after an episode about the theory of Intelligent Design. One woman commented that she'd always feared science and evolution. Somehow she'd gotten the message that curiosity about science was dabbling in things a good Christian shouldn't be curious about.

Imagine Christians and nonbelievers having FEARLESS CONVERSATIONS about the following topics in a place where God shows up every time:

- Angels Among Us: Stories of Miraculous Encounters
- Animal Insights: What Pets Know That We Don't
- The Art of Loss: How Tragedy Can Transform Your Perspective
- Asperger's Syndrome
- Media Bias
- Body Language
- Can God Love a Mess Like Me?

99

- Celebrate Mom
- Children With No Place to Call Home
- Dilemmas
- The End Is Near? Countdown to the Apocalypse
- Follow Your Dreams
- Inside the Gun Debate
- Ghost Hunters
- How to Spot a Liar: Secrets From a Former FBI Agent
- Can Anyone Tell Your Future?
- A Stripper's Journey Out of Hopelessness
- Making Peace With Your Past: A Vietnamese Refugee's Journey
- Life's Myths: What You Believe That's Wrong
- Secrets Learned in Solitary Confinement
- Make the Most of Your Life
- Our Wild, Weird, Wonderful World
- Meth: Stories of Horror and Hope
- Mysteries of Mental Illness
- Can One Religion Have All the Answers?
- Feeling Up When Times Are Down
- The Struggle to Forgive
- Living After Suicide
- Three Cheers for Failure!
- The Upside of a Down Economy
- Our Love Affair With Vampires
- UFOs
- An Encounter With God: A Prime Minister's Supernatural Experience
- What People *Really* Think of Christians
- Triumph Over Trauma
- Eating Disorders
- Amazing Grace: The Mother of the Shooter Finds Healing in the Aftermath of the Amish Schoolhouse Massacre
- The Black and White Truth About Racism
- When Love Hurts: Ending the Cycle of Domestic Violence
- How to Live Before You Die
- The Majesty and Mystery of Nature
- Prayer: Could a Conversation With God Change Your Life?
- How to Stop Doing What You Hate
- Family Secrets
- Imperfect Parents: Making Peace and Moving On
- Hoarding

- Identity Theft
- Islam
- Mormonism
- Hell: Does It Really Exist?
- The Art of Listening

These provocative topics—and many, many more—have attracted a wide variety of people from our community week after week. Every time, people participate in healthy, open dialogue, even when they totally disagree. It's been truly remarkable to witness the power of FEARLESS CONVERSATION in our Lifetree Café experiment.

Spoiler alert: Churches *can* offer endless opportunities for FEARLESS CONVERSATION with any size group. There's no excuse for not offering times to allow people to talk with one another in any setting. It's simply wrong to believe conversations occur only in small groups. Read Chapter 8 to see what we mean.

Jesus-Style **FEARLESS CONVERSATION**

Jesus loved getting people to think. He asked provocative questions, such as "What do you want?" "Where is your faith?" and "Who do you say that I am?" And he often asked just one simple question: "What do you think?"

If you want a fun exercise, find a Bible and highlight all of Jesus' questions. You'll be amazed how often Jesus left people wondering. He wanted people to ponder, to grapple with, to own their faith. He told open-ended parables, leaving people to figure them out on their own.

In one instance, a religious leader who struggled with faith questions was searching for spiritual guidance. Not unlike people today, he had questions. Jesus posited a perplexing idea: "Unless you are born again, you cannot see the Kingdom of God."

"'What do you mean?' exclaimed Nicodemus. 'How can an old man go back into his mother's womb and be born again? […] How are these things possible?'" (John 3:4, 9).

Jesus replied, "For God loved the world so much that he gave his one and only Son, so that everyone who believes in him will not perish but have eternal life" (John 3:16).

No encounter was off limits. Jesus talked to prostitutes. Sick people. Possessed people. Friends. An unproductive fig tree. The wind and waves. Disgruntled religious people. Jesus even had a feisty encounter with the devil. Jesus knew the power that was in him: God's power.

And that same power will help us with our own FEARLESS CONVERSATIONS.

> **I ALSO PRAY THAT YOU WILL UNDERSTAND THE INCREDIBLE GREATNESS OF GOD'S POWER FOR US WHO BELIEVE HIM. THIS IS THE SAME MIGHTY POWER THAT RAISED CHRIST FROM THE DEAD** and seated him in the place of honor at God's right hand in the heavenly realms.
>
> — Ephesians 1:19-20

> What shall we say about such wonderful things as these? **IF GOD IS FOR US, WHO CAN EVER BE AGAINST US?**
>
> — Romans 8:31

As Christians, we often forget that God is on our side. He's with us. He'll never leave us or forsake us. We simply need to be faithful and trust him. He'll give us the words to say—or not to say. FEARLESS CONVERSATION means engaging without fear. Engaging with love.

When Jesus appeared to his disciples after his death and resurrection, he asked, "Why are you frightened? Why are your hearts filled with doubt?"

We used to think Jesus was ticked when he asked these questions. But maybe Jesus was lovingly confronting his disciples instead.

"Look at my hands," Jesus said. "Look at my feet. You can see that it's really me. Touch me and make sure that I am not a ghost, because ghosts don't have bodies, as you see that I do."

We, too, can show our hands and feet to those with doubts and questions. Let's assure them through our own stories and experiences that Jesus is real.

"As he spoke, he showed them his hands and his feet. Still they stood there in disbelief, filled with joy and wonder." (Luke 24:37-41)

People want to be free to ask, wonder, and experience give and take. Jesus gave his friends something to hold on to in the midst of their doubts. You can give those you encounter *you*—your listening ear, gentle touch, and open mind—so they can see Jesus alive in you! What an awesome privilege to be given the same opportunity as the risen Christ!

Our good friend Dave told us this story about how FEARLESS CONVERSATION unfolded at his church:

"Our new church was excited to have the sister of a Christian celebrity come to share her testimony of 1,111 days of sobriety after 37 years of living as a 'serious, hardcore, dedicated, classic, textbook alcoholic.' She flew in from another state with her brother, who was there to serve as her moral support for this, her first public speaking engagement. After a restless Saturday night, our speaker caved in to the temptation of the bottle, and by Sunday morning, she was so inebriated that speaking was out of the question. Our pastor could have swept the incident under the rug, made an excuse, and pulled a classic sermon out of the archives. Instead, he made the bold decision to let her brother explain what had happened, tell a portion of the family's dramatic story, and then use this unexpected turn of events as an opportunity to express real love to this discouraged sister. At the end of the service, worshippers were invited to write notes of love and encouragement to this friend who had just fallen off the wagon."

Dave told us that hundreds of notes poured in and were forwarded to the woman. Here are a few examples of the gracious words of love and encouragement that were offered:

- "I hope _____ and her entire family feel the love and prayers pouring out from this church. This is what real life and real struggles are all about."

- "My heart goes out to _____. I hope she feels the love from this congregation...no shame or contempt here."

- "You are in all our prayers, and our arms are wide open when you decide to come see us again."

This story of radical love in the middle of real-life struggles proved to be one of the most dramatic in this young church's journey. Dozens of people commented that it was the most powerful church service they had ever attended. ACTS OF LOVE transform not only the members of a congregation as they demonstrate God's love, mercy, forgiveness, and grace but also the recipients, who experience grace instead of judgment, love instead of hate, and encouragement instead of shame. "What a joy to be a part of the church when it truly is known by its love," Dave said.

A Travel Parable
From the Shark Cage

We've done a lot of wild things: We've chased tornadoes. Visited cannibals. Peered into exploding volcanoes. Crossed the Drake Passage, the most treacherous seas in the world, on our way to Antarctica. Piloted glaciers in Alaska. Explored submerged Japanese shipwrecks from World War II. Eaten lap-lap in Vanuatu. Some would say it's crazy to do these things. But we consider them calculated risks—exciting, but not deadly.

One particular adventure taught me (Joani) a lot about fear—shark cage diving. We planned to encounter great white sharks in one of the few places on the planet where you can do such things—near Cape Town, South Africa.

We loaded onto a boat equipped with a steel cage capable of holding two humans and a fake wooden seal. (I wouldn't have been fooled by the floppy decoy but the sharks were.) We aimed for a spot close to an island covered with barking, sniffing, smelly seals. They're the reason great whites like to hang out there. They're a scrumptious breakfast, lunch, or dinner for a hungry shark.

The captain briefed us on procedures. I didn't feel too reassured when I noticed he was missing a few fingers. Gulp! Our mission: Don snorkel masks, jump into the cage dangling over the side of the boat, and when the captain yells, "Down! Down! Down!" take a giant gulp of air so we can hold our breath as the sharks take aim at the cage.

The experience was surreal. The giant monsters slammed toward the steel bars of the cage, glaring at us as they swarmed around the cage.

Great white sharks are gnarly, mean, and nasty looking. We stared them in the face as they swam within inches of us. They're creepy, scary, fierce, daunting, scarred, and grisly.

The experience lasted as long as we could hold our breath.

All this sounds terrifying. But here's the truth: We were safe and secure behind those bars. Our captain had done this hundreds of times. We were safe even though it looked like we were defying death.

It was exhilarating!

This example reminds us of FEARLESS CONVERSATIONS. Christians work themselves into a tizzy, scared to death of actually talking to people who hold different opinions. Somehow we're sure we won't emerge unscathed. We fear we'll be eaten alive. We don't trust our Guide, who's been there before. We imagine we're all alone with the sharks. We forget that our captain—our Captain—will be with us.

And we forget how exhilarating a FEARLESS CONVERSATION about faith can be when we experience God in action. Fear not!

E

S

ACT OF LOVE #2 **FEARLESS CONVERSATION**

After a harrowing time, Paul wrote to his friends in Corinth, "We were crushed and overwhelmed beyond our ability to endure, and we thought we would never live through it. In fact, we expected to die. But as a result, we stopped relying on ourselves and learned to rely only on God, who raises the dead. And he did rescue us from mortal danger, and he will rescue us again. **WE HAVE PLACED OUR CONFIDENCE IN HIM, AND HE WILL CONTINUE TO RESCUE US."**

— 2 Corinthians 1:8-10

"**TRUST IN THE LORD WITH ALL YOUR HEART**; do not depend on your own understanding."

— Proverbs 3:5

WHY NOBODY WANTS TO GO TO CHURCH ANYMORE

How to Recognize
FEARLESS
CONVERSATION

FEARLESS CONVERSATION is…

- **seeking to understand.** When practicing this ACT OF LOVE, Christians strive to grasp why someone thinks, feels, or responds a certain way. This skill is not easy. Because we view the world through our own experiences, it requires thinking of others before ourselves—a loving, Jesus-style trait.

  When seeking to understand others, we can deal with real-life issues in a way that keeps relationships intact. After a Lifetree Café episode about same-sex marriage, we received these comments from participants around the country:

  "Difficult subject handled very well."

  "Very good conversation that made me think. It gave me a desire to continue to search what God says about the issue."

  "Very interesting, yet touchy subject. This was discussed without bashing others. Thank you!"

- **listening, *really* listening, before speaking.** Because Christians can be secure in God's truth and the Holy Spirit's support, we don't need to be fearful that our point won't be heard. In fact, when we wag fingers and argue without earning the right to be heard, we miss great opportunities to be Jesus to others.

"Understand this, my dear brothers and sisters: **YOU MUST ALL BE QUICK TO LISTEN, SLOW TO SPEAK, AND SLOW TO GET ANGRY.**"
— James 1:19

107

> "Let your conversation be gracious and attractive **SO THAT YOU WILL HAVE THE RIGHT RESPONSE FOR EVERYONE.**"
>
> — Colossians 4:6

- **asking great questions.** Lame questions are one of the things that give Sunday school curriculum a bad name. (One church planter recently told us that curriculum is a four-letter word!)

  People want to engage their brains and hearts. To make that happen, we must ask great questions—questions that are surprising, specific, and personal, questions that give others a chance to pause.

- **asking "wondering" questions.** Instead of asking yes or no questions about facts, those who love FEARLESS CONVERSATION engage in the art of wondering. Our friend Doug Pollock, author of *God Space*, has perfected this art. When someone says something that contradicts our Christian beliefs, we can ask, "I'm wondering what happened that led you to believe that?" or "I'm wondering what you read that brought you to that conclusion?" In this way, we can be respectfully, relationally curious as we develop a deeper understanding of others.

DO: Here's a sampling of Doug Pollock's "wondering" questions. Take them for a test drive during your next conversation.

- Would you mind sharing with me the greatest piece of wisdom ever passed on to you?
- What do you like most about what you do? least?
- If someone wanted to talk to you about God, how would you like to be approached?
- What images or words come to your mind when you hear the word *evangelism?*
- What is your dream job?
- Why do you think there are so many different religions?
- What conclusions have you come to concerning life after death?

- Have you ever been able to get a handle on what you think your purpose in life is?
- Do you consider yourself to be a Christian?
- Based on your understanding, how does someone become a Christian?
- As you've watched or read the news, what conclusions have you drawn about the nature of humanity?
- Have you ever had an experience in which you felt the presence of God?
- What causes you to struggle the most with the idea of God's existence?

- **allowing others to talk—even in a sermon or Bible study.** Radical as it sounds, churches need to allow time for participants to talk. We know that pastors and other leaders flinch at the thought, but sound education methodology understands that people of all ages can only absorb up to 10 minutes of input at a time. It's true! So to be more effective—and to practice FEARLESS CONVERSATION—we must give others time to discuss, download, grapple, and debrief. All of this helps personalize the point and ensure it will stick.

Norm Wakefield, seminary professor and former pastor, told me (Joani) that he challenges his students to talk more. "For truth to stick, you have to work with it," he said. "The act of verbalizing imprints truth on our mind. It's important to allow people of any age to talk it out. That's how our human minds work. We work it out by talking it out. That's another reason lecturing is so inefficient. I've discovered pastors love to discover something and talk it out."

We wonder what would happen if pastors allowed others the gift of "talking things out" so people could own their faith even more. Sadly, we've professionalized faith to the point where most people fear they'll say the wrong thing. So they say nothing.

Leaders might fear discussions will get off topic or spawn heresy. Don't worry! ("Fear not," remember?) Your point of view and expertise are still valid. By listening to others, you're earning an even greater right to be heard. You, too, can be a valued participant, not a spectator.

If you want something to worry about, consider this: If you're doing all the talking, you can't know what's going on in the heads of your listeners. You may think a quiet congregation or group is tracking with you, but adults are just better at hiding when their minds are wandering. Adults can sit, nodding in seeming agreement, while actually planning their list of errands or thinking about the menu of their favorite restaurant. (One Sunday when we stood after the sermon, we spied a woman's forgotten grocery list in the pew in front of us!)

- **using pair shares.** The simplest and cheapest way to engage everyone at anytime and in any setting—during a sermon, class, or meeting—is simply to ask people to turn to a partner and talk about what you just said. We call this a pair share. (And it isn't the same as turning to a neighbor and saying, "Hi, neighbor" in an attempt at relationship building.)

DO: Ask people to talk with one other person. This concept is easy and free. You don't need the latest technological whiz-bang gizmos. Just ask everyone to turn to a partner and react to what was just said.

That is FEARLESS CONVERSATION. It allows the Holy Spirit to meet people where they are. And it works! We've used pair shares for years with hundreds of thousands of people of all ages.

- **offering nonjudgmental responses.** Too often, we can't stop ourselves from commenting on people's answers. We might say, "Great answer" when we agree. Or "Hmm…not was I was thinking" when they haven't parroted the response we were fishing for. Or "That's interesting" when we're dumbfounded by such a thought.

Stop and think about this. What happens when our answers or ideas or thoughts or experiences are judged? It's likely happened to you countless times in conversations or classrooms. If we're honest, we'll admit we feel slightly superior when a teacher praises us. And we feel shut down when a teacher says, "Not exactly…"

Giving a nonjudgmental response is an art that most of us in the church have not perfected. "Thanks" or "uh-huh" or a nod indicate that we're tracking without shutting down interaction. (And lest you think we're in favor of heresy or free-for-alls, read more in Chapter 8.)

- **trusting the Holy Spirit and believing that God is on our side.** This may be the real missing ingredient in churches today. We have programmed, planned, and prepared down to the minutest detail, leaving no room for God to actually work. Or maybe we haven't planned at all and are completely winging it. The only problem is, we do all the talking and figure God is only speaking through us—and no one else.

FEARLESS CONVERSATION is <u>not</u>...

- **pretending to pay attention.** Some people have mastered this. They look like they're paying attention to what another person is saying, but their mental wheels are spinning a hundred miles an hour. They're already crafting a comeback. Or they're nodding, but their thoughts are actually a hundred miles away. Paying attention is hard work. And with smartphones to distract us, being fully present and attentive to another human being is becoming increasingly rare these days. The simple act of being fully present and engaged can set you apart.

- **having all the answers.** Christians seem to feel the need to present a confident faith with no uncertainties. Or we think that asking a tough question means we're weak in our faith. Or that we must have a full explanation for every one of life's mysteries. It's understandable; to those outside the faith, we don't want to appear ignorant or as if we're living in a fantasy world. But the truth is, people just want to know that we share this journey called life and that even in our thoughts and doubts, we remain anchored in a belief that sustains us and continues to transform our lives.

- **asking questions you already know the answers to.** Bible studies and small groups often only allow for one-way communication. It's much better to let people grapple. They don't want to feel inferior to or less intelligent than the teacher or "expert." If we can remember that we're all working our way through life and that none of us is ever 100 percent right, then our approach to Bible studies, teaching, and ministry blossoms into something truly relational.

- **one person (the pastor, Bible study leader, or Sunday school teacher) doing all the talking.** We know it can be hard to accept, but everything about effective education tells us that students must be actively engaged. (Dig deeper into this in Chapter 8.) There's definitely a place for pastors, teachers, and leaders, but their roles are very different today. It may have been different in an age when people couldn't read or didn't have access to information. But in our interactive, access-to-information-24/7 age, our role as leaders has changed dramatically. For people of any age to own their faith, they must engage in dialogue that gets them to verbalize that faith. FEARLESS CONVERSATIONS can never happen on a one-way street.

> Technique is never value neutral. If you choose lecture as your sole means of delivering information [...] you are in effect saying to your learners that you value what *you* have to say more than what *they* have to say."[1]
> — Sharon L. Bowman, *How to Give It So They Get It*

- **Bible studies for the elite.** We've inadvertently scared off anyone who might actually want to learn more about God, Jesus, and the Bible. Instead of welcoming newcomers, Bible study groups can be perceived as snooty. For those who dare admit they don't know that Exodus is in the Old Testament or have no idea where John 3:16 can be found (and what is "three sixteen" anyway?), Bible studies can be intimidating. We'll never forget the time we were in a Bible study group filled with retired pastors. They spent most of the class impressing their peers with biblical know-how while the rest of us were left in the dust. What regular person wouldn't feel stupid in such a situation?

- **sermons, guest speakers, and panels on controversial topics.** On the surface, this might look fearless. But it's almost always a one-way street for the church's point of view. We're not against the church's point of view. Obviously, the God of the Bible is "the way, the truth, and the life." However, our culture today demands participation in the conversation. One-way communication isn't best to help people see—or, more important, own—the "one way."

- **allowing only "approved" books, music, and options.** It seems farfetched to think that churches would ban certain books and music. But some church bodies are hunkering into a mentality that impels them to dictate "theologically correct" music, books, and curriculum in every church-related venue. Don't believe it? Read on...

Acts of a Suicidal Church

This summer's big regional youth conference has been cancelled. Because of tunes.

The leader of the denominational office notified all the churches in the region that he decided to pull the plug. The reason? Conference organizers had planned to use Christian songs that did not come from the official denominational worship book.

He cited church rules that require the "exclusive use of doctrinally pure agenda" and "theologically correct hymns and materials."

So, what has been gained by the cancellation of the youth conference? Well, the churches' teenagers have been protected from attending a conference and hearing Christian songs penned by "unapproved" Christian composers. Instead, the kids spent the time at home listening to their usual secular songs.

Unfortunately, this is not an isolated case of churches' desperate attempts to cling to their manmade sectarian rules, relics, and soapboxes. They're in survival mode. But their actions amount to acts of institutional suicide.

Most denominations in America are shrinking—some rather precipitously. Financial giving is down. Generally, the influence of the church in American culture is dimming. Faith in the institution of the church is waning, particularly among the young.

In the face of these negative trends, many church bodies have taken on a bunker mentality. They've attempted to isolate, tighten controls, lob grenades at anyone outside their bunker, dig in, and clutch what's left inside.

Some believe their only chance of survival lies in denominational brand distinctiveness. And they're resolved to ride their quaint distinctives to the very end. They've adopted the old Kodak brand mindset: "Our hope resides in clinging to what we've been known for, to what we've always done. If we don't stand for film, what do we stand for?" Kodak old-timers forgot they were really in the picture business, not the film business. Similarly, many in the church have forgotten they're in the faith business, not the doctrinal nit-picking business.

These churches aren't withering because they're not gripping tightly enough to brand distinctives. Their enemy is not other brands, other churches, other believers, other doctrinal nuances. The enemy is much more elemental. The enemy is disbelief.

If we want any hope of reversing troubling church trends, especially among young people, we must focus not on tribal heritage, denominational branding, theological hair-splitting, or pharisaical purity. We must focus on Jesus—and his sacrificial love for us and all people.

HolySoup.com

Now that we've taken a look at what FEARLESS CONVERSATION means, let's dig into some practical ways you can make it work for your church.

Endnote

1. Sharon L. Bowman, *How to Give It So They Get It* (Glenbrook, NV: Bowperson Publishing, 2005), 119.

8 PRACTICAL WAYS TO LOVE WITH FEARLESS CONVERSATION

Your church doesn't have to be the place that offers only **ONE-WAY MONOLOGUES WITH NO ROOM FOR DISCUSSIONS OR QUESTIONS.**

Making FEARLESS CONVERSATIONS happen is a lot easier than you might think. Research and experience have taught us that when you do the things described in this chapter, you'll pave the way for two-way, respectful dialogue. And more than that, you'll pave the path for *real, meaningful, lasting relationships.*

Rest assured, we've put all these ideas into practice and have seen amazing results time after time after time. You can, too!

Assess Your Church's
TEACHING AND SMALL-GROUP SETTINGS

Think of a typical sermon, class, or small group in your church. Read the following chart and ponder: Are your church's trainings mostly in the "great" or "poor" column?

When we read this, we realized most churches' offerings fall into the "poor training" column. Do you agree?

Examples of What Makes for *Great* Training	Examples of What Makes for *Poor* Training
It responds to my needs.	It was too far removed from my interests.
I could see how it applied to me.	I couldn't see how I would use it.
There was a lot of participation.	It was a one-way transmission of information.
I was drawn in quickly.	I soon was in information overload.
The explanations were clear and concise.	There was little to no discussion.
I could relate to the examples.	There was little to no practice.
It applied to my job.	There was little to no feedback to me personally on what I did.
I could ask questions at any time.	The materials were poorly designed.
I didn't feel stupid.	A lot of time was wasted.
I felt I added value to the session.	There was very little I could take back to my job.
There were lots of takeaways I could use.	The content was okay, but the methods for communicating were poor.
It helped me do my work better.	I was a passive listener most of the time.
The session was interactive.	I couldn't understand what was being taught.

I could try out what was taught.	The language and/or jargon lost me.
I got feedback on how I did.	There were very few, if any, examples that I understood.
There was warmth and humor.	It was dull, monotonous, and boring.
I learned a lot from the other participants	There was little or no class interaction with other participants.
The materials were clear and useful.	I was just another body in the course.
I felt respected.	I contributed nothing or little to the session.
There was lots of two-way communication.	I didn't learn much.
There wasn't a lot of time wasted.	I couldn't ask questions when I wanted.

Excerpted from *Telling Ain't Training* by Harold D. Stolovitch and Erica J. Keeps.[1]

Question
HOW MUCH YOU LECTURE

In other words, rethink how much time one person does all the talking.

When you allow everyone to talk, you expand and deepen ownership of the truth. Give everyone a chance to talk and you'll increase your effectiveness exponentially. *If you do this one thing, you'll transform your ministry.* And it's *free!* It doesn't cost anything.

How do you do it? Make everyone a teacher. You've heard the phrase, "The one who learns the most is the teacher." So turn everyone into a teacher.

We learn by talking things out. Our brains process ideas and concepts by talking about them.

Just let everyone talk more.

Leaders and pastors enjoy finding gems of truth in Scripture; they're excited to talk about them and preach about them. What if we instilled that same love of God's Word and discovery in everyone? That happens when we allow other people to join in the conversation (fearlessly, of course!).

Think about it: How do *you* learn best? Take this quick quiz to see where you land.

I learn best when…

Someone who knows something I don't explains and describes it to me.	I dialogue and discuss with someone who knows something I don't.
I observe a demonstration.	I get involved and try things out during a demonstration.
I attend lectures in which an instructor presents information to me.	I attend sessions in which an instructor engages me in a two-way interaction.
There is a lot of detailed content.	There is minimal and meaningful content.
What is presented to me is organized according to the logic of the content.	What is presented to me is organized according to the logic of how I learn.
I am shown how things are done.	I get to try things for myself.
I attend long learning sessions.	I attend short learning sessions.
I am in a formal instructional setting.	I am in an informal work and learning setting.
I am told how things work.	I experience how things work.

Excerpted from *Telling Ain't Training* by Harold D. Stolovitch and Erica J. Keeps.[2]

> Text and oral presentations are not just less efficient than pictures for retaining certain types of information; they are *way* less efficient. If information is presented orally, people remember about 10 percent, tested 72 hours after exposure. That figure goes up to 65 percent if you add a picture.[3]
>
> — John J. Medina, *Brain Rules*

Be Conversational, NOT PRESENTATIONAL

The Internet has opened up a participatory, interactive, two-way street. In fact, when the Internet really exploded was when it moved from just information (1.0) to interaction and connectivity (2.0) and became a dialogue, not a monologue. Imagine how different sermons and lesson plans would be if preachers and teachers built in the concept of a two-way street where everyone embarks on the journey together.

When we ask people why they've left the church and the Sunday morning sermon/teaching time, we hear them ask again and again: "What if it were more of a conversation? What if I could raise my hand and ask a question during the sermon?" Some pastors have begun to expand their sermons to include a Q&A time or have encouraged people to text them their questions during the sermon. That has to be exhilarating, surprising, and a bit threatening to be put on the spot, but for pastors and teachers to be relevant, it's a brilliant idea.

> Imagine the following scene. In one hand I have a pitcher filled with water. In the other I have a glass with its bottom facing upward. What happens when I try to pour water into the glass? Obviously, it spills over the glass and my hand because the inside of the glass is closed off to what is being poured. This physical example of wasted effort is analogous to a trainer trying to pour content into a closed adult learner's mind.[4]
>
> — Harold D. Stolovitch and Erica J. Keeps, *Telling Ain't Training*

Make **ONE POINT**

Dump the three-point linear sermon we've all been trained to deliver. Today we're dealing with the Internet world. Think Web. Think links. Make one point and come at it from multiple directions. Use a variety of methodologies and people will more likely get it.

Group's vacation Bible school material is a powerful example of this. Over a week's time, we immerse kids in multiple experiences to cement one Bible point every day. At week's end, children can recall every day's Bible point, Bible story, and life application. Even years later, children remember the truths from that VBS week.

The idea of clear, one-point learning works in a 20-minute sermon as well as an hour-long class. Making only one point challenges us as leaders to clarify our goals. No more rambling. No more filling up time. An intentional goal of making one point pushes leaders to be better.

ABOLISH Fill-in-the-Blank Sermons and Classes

We've talked about this already, but it bears repeating. Think about it this way: Do you ever have effective conversations with people by expecting them to guess what you're trying to say? Neither have we.

Think **SMALL**

If you want people to open up and participate, it's best to allow them to talk in smaller groups. How many of us have watched a leader pose a question to a group—and cringed when no one spoke up? If we're serious about involving others, allow as many people as possible to converse. Most of the time we recommend forming groups of no more than four. Why? Any larger and it becomes public speaking. And the number one fear of people anywhere in the world is public speaking. So to ease the fear of sharing, think small.

FORM GROUPS of Two, Three, Four, or Six

How many times have you been told in church meetings to "get together in a small group" only to find yourself in a group of 10 to 12 in which only two or three people talked?

Be clear and specific about keeping your groups small. This allows the entire group to discuss more questions and ensures that everyone participates.

Groups of six provide flexibility. They can morph into three pairs or two trios or remain all together. If you're running out of time, have people answer in pairs instead of trios or sixes to make sure each person has time to talk.

By the way, it's a myth that interactivity works only with small audiences. We've created environments for intimate conversation in groups of more than 2,000 simply by asking them to form groups of two, three, four, or six. Right there, right then.

Plan for ALL-GROUP REPORT BACKS

This holds people accountable, plus it gives you and the group the opportunity to hear lots of different ideas. After people share in pairs or small clusters, ask for a few responses from the crowd.

Ask GOOD QUESTIONS

Move beyond questions that prompt "yes" or "no" answers to questions that dig into "why," "what," and "how." Good questions ask people to share what they really think and make it safe and acceptable for them to do so. Good questions don't have right or wrong answers; instead, they allow people to share their thoughts and stories without feeling pressure to say the right thing. Good questions even allow for people to ask more questions.

Here are some examples of good questions:

- How does _____ make you feel?
- What questions does _____ raise for you?
- What has your experience taught you about _____?
- What has caused you to change your mind about _____?
- What do you think might happen if _____?
- What happened to you this week that reminded you that _____?

Encourage People to
TELL THEIR OWN STORIES

Asking people to "tell about a time when…" encourages them to consider how topics apply to them personally. And when others respond by listening intently, relationships flourish. This simple technique has made our Lifetree Café experiences irresistible to everyone involved.

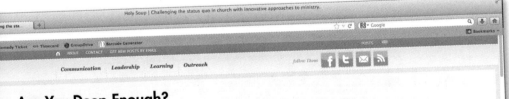

Are You Deep Enough?

"Your ministry [teaching, preaching, Bible studies, curriculum, small group, etc.] isn't deep enough."

It's a critique I hear from time to time. Usually not from participants. But from onlooking ministry leaders.

I've wondered, what do they mean by "deep"? When I've probed, "deep" seems to mean dense information, lots of historical detail, many Bible verses, theological complexity, and a dose of Greek.

I often wonder how today's depth-finders would have evaluated Jesus' ministry. Would he have passed their tests?

I suspect the depth Jesus sought was less about information and more about personal transformation. What he really craved was deep personal relationships with him and the Father.

Personal relationships—including, and especially, relationships with Jesus—are just that: personal. They're not mass-produced in a factory. Or a lecture hall.

Jesus-style depth comes when a person experiences the very presence of God, reaches deeply within, reflects, makes a personal discovery, and grows.

Jesus went deep with his colorful stories, with his probing questions, and with his fully engaging experiences.

Do you want a ministry that goes deep?

- Tell a good story...without always revealing your own spiritual interpretation.

- Ask open-ended, soul-searching questions, ones that each individual must plumb deeply and address individually.

- Involve people in captivating experiences. Wash their feet. Engage all of their senses. Allow God some space to act.

Think like a scuba dive master. You don't help your divers go deep by standing on the surface and spraying them with a big hose. You help them go deep when you allow them to go beneath the surface to personally discover the wonders of God's creation.

HolySoup.com

Choose Scripture
CAREFULLY

Provide well-selected, surprising Scriptures that cause deep thought even among seasoned Christians.

Include POIGNANT
PRAYER TIME

Allow time for God to speak. Listen as well as talk. Communication with God is also a two-way street.

Ask for OTHER POINTS
OF VIEW

After our years of experimenting with Lifetree Café, we've learned that other points of view are out there (even among Christians). Sadly, the church is known for shutting down people with different ideas. But the truth is, the more we allow people to express their points of view, the more we telegraph openness and acceptance of them as people.

123

Soup | Challenging the sta...   Holy Soup | Challenging the status quo in church with innovative approaches to ministry.

holysoup.com

Visited ∨   Remedy Ticket   Timecard   GroupDrive   Barcode Generator

ABOUT   CONTACT   GET NEW POSTS BY EMAIL

Communication   Leadership   Learning   Outreach

follow Thom

How to Silence Your People

"Pastors, preach the word boldly and shut the mouths of your listeners!"

That was an actual comment from a pastor in response to one of my blog posts. My article encouraged pastors to enhance their preaching with effective communication techniques—such as those that Jesus used. These include listening to your people and encouraging people's questions and dialogue.

This pastor's comment reflects a general attitude that pervades some church staffs. The approach seems to be, "I'm the ministry professional. That means it's my job to do the talking. And it's your job to shut up."

Most church leaders aren't as blunt as the pastor quoted above. But the attitude often leaks out in more subtle ways.

I understand how this desire to silence the people becomes attractive. Much of what church leaders hear is negative or ill-informed. It can be exhausting to listen to that stuff.

And, the urge to exclusively dominate all communication is often tied closely to a minister's sense of identity: "I'm the one who went to theological school. I feel called to teach and preach. My calling is not to sit and listen to people who are not called."

And for others it's a matter of time management. "I have a lot to say, a lot to share. I simply don't have time to listen or engage in give-and-take."

But I fear this effort to muzzle the people is hurting the cause. It implies that the professional Christians are the only ones who have answers or have a real connection to God. That's the same kind of misguided elitism that fueled the Reformation some 500 years ago.

And, shaping the church as a place for one-way communication leads to an anemic, passive enterprise. The paid professionals do the talking, share their faith, and perform the ministry. The attendees simply sit in a pew, stay quiet, and do nothing.

In addition, this approach tarnishes its practitioners into poor leaders. They become isolated, out of touch with real people, and disconnected from real life issues.

Listen

Rather than looking for ways to "shut the mouths of your listeners," here are some simple ways to open a conversation that leads to faith growth and effective ministry.

- Provide opportunities for people to publicly tell about how God is working in their lives. Let them speak, interview them, or show their stories on video.

- Grant time in classes, studies, and sermons for people to talk and listen to one another.

- Solicit feedback. It's how you grow. It's how you know your people. Ask people how your message touched them. Use comment cards and occasional surveys. Welcome the use of performance reviews.

- Visit and listen to people on their own turf—in their homes, workplaces, schools, and hangouts.

- Listen to people outside your peer group. Many pastors say they read and listen to only one group—other pastors. This leads to dangerous inbreeding. Seek out the voices of thought leaders in other fields.

Listen. This doesn't mean you should be silenced. It simply means you'll be more effective when you do speak.

HolySoup.com

WHY NOBODY WANTS TO GO TO CHURCH ANYMORE

Include
EXPERTS' INSIGHTS

We can all benefit from experts. Sometimes that expert can be you or someone in your congregation. Sometimes it can be people far removed from the church, even non-Christians. Of course, we always turn to the Bible for expert insight, as well.

Provide
INTERESTING DATA

Remember the logical thinkers. Many people are wired for data. They're interested in it; they love to analyze it. Provide a balanced viewpoint by providing relevant facts, statistics, and research.

Use PHRASES SUCH AS...

"I wonder..."

Our friend Doug Pollock describes himself as a recovering evangelist who has learned the power of the phrase "I wonder." This simple phrase gives people permission to speak their minds without being defensive or guarded. (See Chapter 7 for examples of great wondering questions.)

"Could it be..."

This is a great phrase to use when you disagree with someone. Instead of flatly stating your opinion, simply phrase it as a question beginning with "Could it be...?" By asking a question instead of making a declaration, you'll open the door to conversation instead of shutting it.

"Some people say..."

Referring to the opinions of others (or even your own, in third person) helps to maintain common ground and avoid personal conflict. It allows the other person to respond to an idea without associating that idea with you or a specific person.

Encourage **THINKING**

The church is notorious for suppressing thinking. One time, a pastor visited Lifetree Café and had the privilege of sitting with someone who didn't believe in prayer. By the end of the hour, people had really grappled with prayer—what it is and how it works. But the pastor wasn't pleased. "I don't like all these questions because I have the answers. It's a waste of time to ask so many questions," he told us. Not surprisingly, his church never flourished.

Dumb Questions Heard in Church

No wonder most people walk away from church with little to show for it.

Recent Barna research revealed that most people (61 percent) cannot recall gaining any spiritual insights the last time they attended church.[5]

Part of the problem stems from uninspiring content—answering questions no one is asking. (I recently sat through a sermon about theological speculations on vegetarian dinosaurs.)

And part of the problem has to do with garden-variety poor teaching methodologies. Teachers fail to engage their people in learning.

The best teachers and preachers know that communication/learning is a two-way street. People need to actively engage in the process if they are to gain new insights.

To help facilitate this type of engagement, many teachers ask questions. But all too often their questions fail to evoke learning or engagement. Most of these well-intended but poorly crafted questions seek factual recall. They're close-ended questions—the type that beg a pat answer, usually predetermined by the teacher.

Asking a close-ended question to a room full of people and waiting for one smarty-pants to cough up the one correct answer is a hopeless waste of time.

This poor teaching methodology is not limited to children's ministry. An adult colleague of mine told me of a veteran church teacher who baited his class with a question that sought his pet, pat answer. He finally wrote his predetermined answer on the board.

My friend said, "From there he lectured for 45 minutes. We weren't really discussing or thinking—just regurgitating. Needless to say, I will not be going back."

If you wish to engage your people—of any age—ask open-ended questions. Ask questions that evoke a different, thoughtful response from each person.

For examples of good questions, go through the Gospels and underline every question Jesus asked. You'll find an abundance of open-ended questions that caused his people to think, grapple, and make personalized discoveries. Examples:

- "Why do you doubt?"
- "Why worry about a speck in your friend's eye when you have a log in your own?"

If you want the kind of ministry that makes a difference in the lives of your people, dig into questions that matter. And ask questions that cause your people to plumb deeply and reflect on what God is stirring in their souls.

HolySoup.com

Set Ground Rules That
FOSTER RESPECT AND CIVILITY

It's perfectly acceptable to tell a group what kind of conversation is expected.

For example, in youth ministry we declare "no putdown zones" to create an atmosphere of emotional safety. Be wary of sharp wit and snarky humor. Those who talk that way are simply veiling their insecurities. In a culture of cyber-bullying and face-to-face bullying, we can make our churches a welcome haven of kindness. And don't think these ground rules are meant only for children and teenagers. Adults need reminding, too.

In Lifetree Café, which is filled with people of different ages and widely varying ideas, we intentionally talk about hot topics that could lead to conflict. We acknowledge issues that are especially controversial or touchy. Then we explain that we're about to have a respectful conversation. To our delight, we've found that even the most volatile topics can be discussed respectfully when the leader sets appropriate ground rules.

We believe people *want* FEARLESS CONVERSATIONS. After an episode called "The Gun Debate," one person wrote on Facebook: "It was a great event tonight. Lots of opinions and lots of listening. Nobody shouted, and I think we left with respect for each other. We need to stop watching the news and *talk* with people."

Our churches can become places for civil, respectful, loving conversations among people of all ages.

Make Your Point in Chunks—10 MINUTES OR LESS

Researchers have found that the human brain, regardless of age, can absorb no more than 10 minutes of information at a time.

And our attention peaks at the beginning and at the end. Think about it. When someone says, "In closing…" what happens? People snap to attention.

The secret is to create lots of beginnings and endings. Work toward a "discovery" instead of being in "tell" mode all the time.

127

Tackle Tough Subjects
HEAD ON

We've been slammed for designing activities that allow kids to talk about hard things. For example, in our Holy Land Adventure VBS we showed kids pictures of a spider, a school, and a gravestone. They were asked to talk about what they feared most among those three things. Some teachers said picturing a cemetery headstone is too scary for kids. But their greatest fears have to do with death—the death of a parent, grandparent, friend, or pet. If they can't talk about their greatest fears in church, where can they?

Another complaint came from someone who said we shouldn't use Babylon as the setting for our Holy Land Adventure VBS because it was a godless city. Instead of concentrating on God's almighty power in delivering Daniel from a fiery furnace and a lions' den, she fixated on the pagan culture.

Now is the time to cling to God's almighty power! Fear not!

Holy Soup | Challenging the status quo in church with innovative approaches to m...

Holy Soup | Challenging the sta...

holysoup.com

Most Visited   Remedy Ticket   Timecard   GroupDrive   Barcode Generator

ABOUT   CONTACT   GET NEW POSTS BY EMAIL

follow Thom

POSTS   MY

Communication   Leadership   Learning   Outreach

Tackle the Touchy Subjects—and Survive

The planned discussion on same-sex marriage really riled him up. He feared the forum might attract "seekers" then lead them astray.

He contacted his pastor and asked, "Why are we exposing unbelievers with no biblical backing to the worst of false doctrine?"

Though this man never attended any of the discussions on controversial topics, he left his church because he said dealing with these issues was "nothing short of compromise."

Dealing with controversial subjects at church is, well, controversial. Many churches follow one of two approaches—neither of which is healthy.

- Some church leaders and teachers choose to simply avoid touchy topics. They fear people will disagree and walk away mad.

- Others attempt to shut down discussion (and thinking) about controversial issues with a monologue from the bully pulpit. They dispense the "right answers" and walk away.

Many reject the idea of hearing from those with differing views. The man cited above said, "I just don't see anything beneficial in bringing obvious wolves in sheep's clothing to deceive the sheep and then gobble up those who are already lost."

I'm afraid this fellow would have been really peeved with Jesus, who not only listened to those with differing views, but actually employed one such "wolf" among his 12 associates. Throughout his ministry, Jesus did not hide from touchy topics. He did not shun or silence those who held opposing views. He knew his truth would stand up well in the marketplace of ideas.

The church of today would do well to follow Jesus' example. We must demonstrate that our faith is relevant to all of life, no matter how controversial or difficult the issues. And we must admit that we cannot shield our people from touchy topics. If we don't deal with these issues within the church, our people will simply talk about them outside the church without the benefit of a scriptural perspective. How could that be a better alternative?

Navigating Gnarly Stuff

With Lifetree Café, we often tackle touchy subjects. After several years of creating content for these weekly discussions, we've learned some things about navigating controversial subjects in a Christian environment. Here are some of the secrets:

1. **Set a respectful tone.** At the beginning, acknowledge that the issue is a hot one. Mention that people hold widely differing views on the topic. Do not disparage or belittle those who think differently than you. Establish that this will be a time for a respectful exploration of the issues.

2. **Train your people how to differ.** Express the expectation that people may disagree but will do so in a manner that is friendly and loving. Ask everyone to listen to others without interrupting, passing hasty judgment, or plotting vengeful retorts. Encourage people to share their perspectives and stories in positive ways. Incidentally, this will also prepare your people to interact and glow their faith when they're out in the world.

3. **Allow give and take.** Touchy topics—even those you believe have only One True Side—need to be aired in an environment of interaction. One loud voice at the microphone rarely settles anything. Allow differing views. Encourage questions. Engage people in conversation. This can even be done during sermon times with large groups of people. Simply ask thought-provoking questions and provide some time for people to talk in pairs or threes or fours.

129

4. Let the Scriptures speak. Inject relevant Scripture into the discussion—not as a proof text but as a resource and light. Resist the temptation to contort the Scripture into saying something more than it actually says. Let your people explore how the Scripture may apply to touchy topics. And if different passages provide different perspectives, encourage your people to grapple with those contrasting perspectives.

5. Trust the Holy Spirit. Pray. Invite God into the discussion. Incorporate God's Word. Air differing views. Even allow Judas to speak. Then let the Holy Spirit do what the Holy Spirit does best. Have confidence in the power of God's truth to prevail in the hearts of your people.

HolySoup.com

Design Experiences That
ALLOW DISCOVERY

Group has built its core innovations around experiential (R.E.A.L.) learning. From service projects and field trips to in-class and in-church experiences, using experiential learning techniques will increase your effectiveness and people's "discovery factor" by up to 90 percent.

People are wired differently, so it's important to design experiences for all types of learners. Some are extroverted conversationalists who love to talk. Others are introverted. Some prefer logic and statistics, while others are more driven by emotion. Some like to sit and stay, while others like to keep moving. So make sure to include all kinds of experiences.

Engage EMOTIONS

Never in a manipulative way, but in a Jesus-style way. A way that allows people to express how they really feel, based on their own experiences and conclusions. A great way to tap into genuine, raw emotions is to…

RELATE STORIES,
Not Concepts

Use story power. Live stories as well as stories on film create shared experiences. And be sure to use video to do what video does best: engage emotions. Don't use a talking head to convey a message if you want that message to stick.

Jesus knew people love a good story. Matthew 13:34 tells us that "Jesus always used stories and illustrations like these when speaking to the crowds. In fact, he never spoke to them without using such parables."

Watch for this when you're listening to a sermon. People literally lean forward when someone is telling a story instead of preaching a concept or doctrine.

Here's a no-fail way to help people connect life with faith: Make it personal. People can argue about nearly everything, but they can't argue with your personal story. Most people are comfortable talking about their experiences, and their stories are immediately engaging. They're relevant to everyone; there's no "right" answer. People's stories aren't about concepts; they're about the *real* experiences of *real* people.

When people are asked to tell about a time they feel God protected them or to tell about a time they wondered where God was in the midst of pain, God suddenly becomes very relevant.

Bring Back Stories

Unfortunately, we live in an age in which story has been pushed from its biblical frontline prominence to a bench on the sidelines and then condescended to as 'illustration' or 'testimony' or 'inspiration.' Our contemporary unbiblical preference, both inside and outside the church, is for information over story. We typically gather impersonal (pretentiously called 'scientific' or 'theological') information, whether doctrinal or philosophical or historical, in order to take things into our own hands and take charge of how we will live our lives. And we commonly consult outside experts to interpret the information for us. But we don't live our lives by information; we live them in relationships in the context of a personal God who cannot be reduced to formula or definition, who has designs on us for justice and salvation.[8]

— Eugene H. Peterson, *Eat This Book*

Use Stories as
METAPHORS

Jesus used parables when he wanted to make a point. Metaphors ignite our imaginations. They engage our hearts and minds.

God created us to draw deeper meaning from our day-to-day lives and experiences. R.E.A.L. learning creates parable experiences. Instead of just listening to a story, people experience something, connect it with Scripture, and draw meaning from it. For example, tearing a paper doll and taping it back together helps people understand and remember the power of hurtful or kind words.

CONNECT the Dots

Experiential learning allows people to make their own discoveries in those moments when things click into place and they think, "Ah-ha!" They found it; they own it.

A Group Workcamp is a week packed with experiences and relationships, and it provides countless ways for teens and their leaders to connect the dots between service and faith. Every evening during the week, campers participate in programs that are famous for bringing together all that they've experienced—not through a sermon or somebody telling them what to think, but through a kaleidoscope of prayer stations, interactive drama, hands-on experiences, and a lot of FEARLESS CONVERSATION. Much of that conversation revolves around debriefing or downloading to connect the dots between faith and what they've been doing all week. It's a week overflowing with discovery, ah-ha's, insights, and ownership.

Stay **FOCUSED ON JESUS**

We think Eugene Peterson said it best: "When we submit our lives to what we read in Scripture, we find that we are not being led to see God in our stories but our stories in God's. God is the larger context and plot in which our stories find themselves."[10]

Learn How to **MOVE CONVERSATIONS FORWARD**

Once people start talking in groups of two to six, how do you get them to stop?

- Use an attention-getting device. Our favorite is a wooden train whistle. It gets people's attention without annoying them.

- Warn people that they have 30 seconds to wrap up their conversations.

- Say, "Whoever is talking now will be the last person to share."

- Hold up one hand (to signal stop), and wait until you get everyone's attention.

- If you're playing background music, stop or fade the music to signal it's time to stop.

133

Practice the Art of
LEADING
INTERACTIVE
EXPERIENCES

How long should you let people talk?

Gauge the time by tuning into the group. Watch the people and where they are in the conversation. Some groups will finish right away; some groups will want to keep talking. Over time you'll develop a sense for this and find the right balance. It's an art and a skill, and the more you do it, the better you'll get at it.

When it makes sense to do so, tell the group how much time they'll have to talk. For example, if pairs have one minute to share, their conversation will be very different from the one they would have if they were given 10 minutes.

Warning: From up front, small-group conversations always seem to be going more slowly than they actually are. That's simply because the facilitator isn't involved in them. That's why people who are new to this often make the mistake of not allowing adequate sharing time.

Although we were bored or confused by our teachers and professors when we were students, as instructors and trainers we tend to repeat the practices we hated in others. [...] We can break away from boring, unproductive practices by focusing on our learners as adults with the same sorts of needs, concerns, desires, fears, frustrations, quirks, ambitions, capabilities, and personal priorities that we have.[11]
— Harold D. Stolovitch and Erica J. Keeps, *Telling Ain't Training*

Use "**COMMON SENSES**"

God created us as multisensory beings. So tap into that when creating environments for FEARLESS CONVERSATION. Find ways to engage all the senses, including taste and touch.

Here's an example of one of our most popular activities that works with any size group—it's a multi-sensory exploration of Psalm 34:8: "Taste and see that the Lord is good." We give people a steak sauce to taste and then ask them to list every single ingredient they can discern. After the exercise, we make a common list of ingredients that everyone in the group could discern, then we compare it to the actual (and much longer and surprising) list of ingredients in the steak sauce. Then we ask people why they couldn't discern all the tastes in the sauce, and we talk about what it means to have a "trained palette" that can pick out a broader range of ingredients in things like steak sauce. We next ask what we'd have to do to "improve our palette" when we taste what God is like. It's an unforgettable lesson, and it's the sensory experience that makes it so memorable.

Use "**TANGIBLE TAKEAWAYS**"

Jesus used parables to build bridges from people's lives to spiritual truths. He also used bread, wine, water, sheep, fig trees, coins, and mustard seeds—concrete, touchable, familiar objects—to link people to spiritual truths. Things can be powerful reminders of meaningful experiences and ideas. We call these things tangible takeaways.

For children in our vacation Bible school programs, we've found some amazing tools to help kids connect everyday objects with spiritual truths. Today millions of "Bible Memory Buddies" are in the hands of kids. They may look like toys, but they shouldn't be so quickly dismissed. Each one triggers memories of spiritual truths in each child's mind. We've heard countless stories of kids recalling biblical principles years after experiencing VBS.

Every year in our Workcamp program for youth, we build meaning into some tangible takeaway. It might be a nail, a wristband, or a rag that becomes a reminder of the spiritual transformation that happened that week.

And tangible takeaways are just as powerful with adults. Here are some stories from Lifetree Café as examples:

- Tim reached into his pocket and pulled out a metal rainbow charm with the word *dream* engraved on it. He had received it months earlier at a Lifetree program about the importance of following our dreams. He placed the charm on the table and said, "I don't go anywhere without this. Even when I forget it in my pocket and it clinks around in the dryer, I find it and make sure I take it with me as a reminder to follow God's lead to follow my dreams."

- One woman came to a Lifetree episode called "Overcoming Life's Obstacles." We didn't see her again for six months and thought she'd lost interest. But when she returned, she told us she'd been in treatment for breast cancer. To our amazement, she said that throughout her treatment she had kept a playing card she received during that episode. She pulled the card from her purse and told us that it symbolized how we can't choose the cards we're dealt, but we *can* control our attitudes. She chose God and prayer to get through her battle with cancer, and the tangible takeaway from Lifetree helped her along the way.

> The groups in the multisensory environments always do better than the groups in the unisensory environments. They have more accurate recall. Their recall has better resolution and lasts longer, evident even 20 *years* later. Problem-solving improves. In one study, the group given multisensory presentations generated more than 50 percent more creative solutions on a problem-solving test than students who saw unisensory presentations. In another study, the improvement was more than 75 percent![12]
> — John J. Medina, *Brain Rules*

Find Ways to
AFFIRM OTHERS

People never tire of being encouraged, thanked, or sincerely complimented. Years ago we led a workshop on the keys to a successful youth group meeting. We said that affirmation was the one key that would keep kids coming back. They're usually not even aware that it's happening, but it leaves them eager for more.

The most profound example of affirmation and encouragement happens every summer at our Workcamps. At the beginning of the week, more than 25,000 workcampers each get a manila envelope with their name on it. The envelope is full of blank "care cards." Throughout the week, each camper is challenged to write a positive and uplifting note to each person in his or her crew every day. By the end of the week, every envelope is stuffed with affirming messages that show how God worked through each person that week. Since the inception of Group Workcamps, care cards remain one of the favorite ingredients of the Workcamp experience. Years later we hear from people who have kept their care cards and are still affirmed by them. People can't get too much encouragement. We firmly believe that's how God works.

And affirmation works with any age. At Lifetree Café, people may not be able to articulate what was special about their time together, but they're affirmed throughout the hour. We say, "Thank you for sharing," "Thank you for taking the risk," "Thank you for having a civil conversation."

Affirmation is one way to reflect Jesus' love. We believe it's what makes ministry magnetic.

Endnotes

1. Harold D. Stolovitch and Erica J. Keeps, *Telling Ain't Training* (Alexandria, VA: American Society for Training and Development, 2002), 44-45.

2. Ibid., 7.

3. John J. Medina, *Brain Rules: 12 Principles for Surviving and Thriving at Work, Home, and School* (Seattle, WA: Pear Press, 2008), 234.

4. Harold D. Stolovitch and Erica J. Keeps, *Telling Ain't Training* (Alexandria, VA: American Society for Training and Development, 2002), 47.

5. The Barna Group, "What People Experience in Churches," January 9, 2012, http://www.barna.org/congregations-articles/556-what-people-experience-in-churches?q=gaining+spiritual+insight+church.

6. John J. Medina, *Brain Rules: 12 Principles for Surviving and Thriving at Work, Home, and School* (Seattle, WA: Pear Press, 2008), 89.

7. Harold D. Stolovitch and Erica J. Keeps, *Telling Ain't Training* (Alexandria, VA: American Society for Training and Development, 2002), 46.

8. Eugene H. Peterson, *Eat This Book* (Grand Rapids, MI: Eerdmans Publishing, 2006), 41-42.

9. Peter Guber, "The Inside Story," *Psychology Today*, March 25, 2011, http://www.psychologytoday.com/articles/201103/the-inside-story.

10. Eugene H. Peterson, *Eat This Book* (Grand Rapids, MI: Eerdmans Publishing, 2006), 44.

11. Harold D. Stolovitch and Erica J. Keeps, *Telling Ain't Training* (Alexandria, VA: American Society for Training and Development, 2002), 46.

12. John J. Medina, *Brain Rules: 12 Principles for Surviving and Thriving at Work, Home, and School* (Seattle, WA: Pear Press, 2008), 208.

9

Throughout our lives we've continually STEPPED OUT OF OUR COMFORT ZONES.

Our experiment with Lifetree Café has been no exception. It's a weekly exercise in GENUINE HUMILITY. Over the past five years, we've interviewed and had spiritual conversations with every kind of person imaginable —religious experts, politicians, UFO abductees, ghost hunters, cancer survivors, pet psychics, famous authors, counselors, tragedy survivors, humanitarians, Bible scholars, vampire fanatics, researchers, scientists, and scores of regular people journeying through life.

Regularly rubbing shoulders with people who are different from us offers amazing opportunities to practice Jesus-style humility.

One great example of this was the day we met Rose Elizabeth.

We traveled to Washington, D.C. to join our friend Doug, who'd arranged an interview with the father of one of his coworkers. The father had just revealed that he had become…she. We knew transgenderism would be a fascinating topic to discuss at Lifetree Café.

I (Joani) remember knocking on the door of a modest home in a D.C. suburb. I'd never had any connections with anyone claiming to be a transgender. I didn't know what to expect, and I had butterflies in my stomach. Honestly, the whole concept rattled my sensibilities. I had to shake my prejudices and ask God to give me a giant dose of acceptance. I prayed for a humble and loving heart.

The door opened. We were warmly greeted by a smiling, husky-voiced person wearing a perfect pageboy wig. Rose Elizabeth made us feel at home as we set up the camera and settled in for the interview. For the next few hours, Rose Elizabeth revealed his/her lifelong struggles with feeling like a woman trapped in a man's body.

Now, I don't know how stuff like this happens, but I do know God loves Rose Elizabeth. We had to suspend our "we're better than you" attitudes. We met Rose Elizabeth on common ground as people searching for peace, love, and God's wisdom.

God truly reached into this unique encounter. I believe God wanted us to demonstrate acceptance, love, understanding, curiosity, respect, and GENUINE HUMILITY. God used Rose Elizabeth to teach us all those things. And we're thankful for that. God also taught us that a servant's heart doesn't always come easily or naturally.

The Lifetree Café episode "When He Becomes She" gave communities everywhere a chance to reach a group of people who are often misunderstood, outcast, and longing for acceptance. What transpired during those hours would fill another book! God showed up as people reached out in GENUINE HUMILITY to love others.

Lifestyle differences aren't the only differences that call us to show GENUINE HUMILITY. Maybe some of the hardest differences for us to confront as Christians are differences in beliefs. In Lifetree Café, we've come face to face with Muslims, Mormons, conspiracy theorists, UFOlogists, psychics, and many more people who don't view the world through the same lenses we do.

These days, it's rare for Christians to invite people with differing beliefs to grapple together. It's much more common to try to prove others wrong. We recently experienced a Lifetree episode called "Mormons: Christian? Cult? What Do They Really Believe?" One of the Mormons in attendance commented: "This was a surprise. Thank you for the respectful conversation. We're usually ambushed."

What does that say about Christians' reputation?

What's So Compelling About
GENUINE HUMILTY?

GENUINE HUMILITY requires us to "do unto others as we would have them do unto us." Would you want to be invited to someone's home only to have the host tell you that everything you think and do is wrong? We all have flaws and misdirected beliefs. We're all sinners. But most of us don't respond well when we're impugned rather than loved.

It can be challenging to relinquish control and refrain from setting ourselves up as experts, especially if we've poured a lifetime into theological training and/or years of Bible studies and discipleship courses. All those things are good, but no one likes a know-it-all. Plus, setting ourselves up as Bible gurus can produce the ugly side effects of pride and ego, which have become poison in the church.

To exhibit GENUINE HUMILITY, we must admit "we're all in this together." As humans, we're *all* on this journey of life. We must admit we don't have all the answers. When we show we're as eager and open to learn as those who don't have a relationship with Jesus, we invite others on this exciting God-journey. By asking questions we become more like Jesus. Even though Jesus is God, he asked loads of questions and valued grappling and discovery, always sure of his relationship with God the Father.

Remember, we live in an age of immediate access to abundant information. People aren't hungering for information. They crave authentic, humble, Jesus-centered relationships.

Jesus-Style
GENUINE HUMILITY

Imagine having supper with your friends and Jesus. You're intrigued and wonder a lot about the one who claims to be God. You watch Jesus get up from the table, take off his robe, wrap a towel around his waist, and pour water into a basin. What's he up to? It's awkward, weird, mysterious, and a bit off-putting. He moves from one person to the next, washing each person's feet and gently drying them with a towel. Gross. Not surprisingly,

141

Peter protests. Jesus responds, "You don't understand now what I am doing, but someday you will" (John 13:7).

Do any of us really understand the magnitude of Jesus' actions? He's God, for heaven's sake! He shouldn't have to stoop so low. But he does. In every way, in everything he did, Jesus stooped so low in order to serve us so we could be with him forever.

The night of the foot washing, Jesus also said, "Do you understand what I was doing? You call me 'Teacher' and 'Lord,' and you are right, because that's what I am. And since I, your Lord and Teacher, have washed your feet, you ought to wash each other's feet. I have given you an example to follow. Do as I have done to you. I tell you the truth, slaves are not greater than their master. Nor is the messenger more important than the one who sends the message. Now that you know these things, God will bless you for doing them" (John 13:12-17).

So much transpired that night. In the midst of the events before Jesus' brutal death, he reminded his friends that their ultimate purpose was to be like him: "So now I am giving you a new commandment: Love each other. Just as I have loved you, you should love each other. Your love for one another will prove to the world that you are my disciples" (John 13:34-35).

GENUINE HUMILITY as Jesus lived it was wrapped in love and service to others. If the God of the universe could come to earth as a tiny, helpless baby who grew up and gave his life for us, is it too much to ask that we strive to give our lives away in love? That we never think of ourselves as better than others?

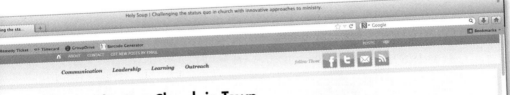

Ramedy Ticket   Timecard   GroupDrive   Barcode Generator

ABOUT   CONTACT   GET NEW POSTS BY EMAIL

POSTS

Communication   Leadership   Learning   Outreach

follow Thom

To Become the Best Church in Town

"Our church has the best youth ministry in town."

"Everybody knows we offer the best children's ministry in the city."

"Our vision is to be the best church in the area."

Over the last ten years, I've heard statements like these with increasing frequency. Is this a good thing? Does our desire to serve God with excellence naturally lead us to want to be the best in town? Is the "best" classification the most honorable way to measure our success and effectiveness?

Most people probably view the quest for best as a helpful ambition. Driving to be better and better, at any endeavor, raises the level of quality for all. Right? Competition makes everyone better. Right? In many ways, that's true.

But what's necessary to be "best"? In any competitive field, in order to have winners you must have losers. In order to be best, you must conquer the others.

And that's where the quest for best begins to turn ugly, especially in the church.

In the church, this spirit of bestfulness and competitiveness leads to pridefulness. This has not gone unnoticed by the public. A non-churched mom I interviewed said, "Churches today just want to be bigger and better than the next one. That's not what church is supposed to be about."

Yet, the quest for best seems intoxicating. Church gurus advise congregations to find something they can be best at in the community. "What makes you stand out among the others?" they ask. The trouble is, we're not called to stand out. We're called to stand behind.

In Mark 9 we see the disciples arguing about who stood out as the best disciple. Jesus confronted their quest for best. He said, "Anyone who wants to be first must be the very last, and the servant of all" (Mark 9:35, NIV). In other words, we're not called to stand out. We're called to stand behind those we're called to serve.

If a church is not called to be the best in town, what is it called to be? It's called to serve. Humbly. It's called to touch lives with God's love, one by one. It's called to be faithful where God has placed it.

No disciple is called to conquer the other disciples in a quest to be best.

Jesus illustrated and summed up his lesson on humble servanthood by picking up one small child and urging his disciples to do the same, to faithfully welcome the small.

It's not the kind of pursuit that will jetison a church to anybody's Best 100 list.

HolySoup.com

No passage sums up Jesus' example of
GENUINE HUMILITY better than Philippians 2:1-11.
Use this Scripture passage to rate your level of GENUINE
HUMILITY. Then rate your church. How does it score?

IS THERE ANY ENCOURAGEMENT FROM BELONGING TO CHRIST?

You Hardly Ever ⟵――――――――――⟶ Most of the Time
Your Church Hardly Ever ⟵――――――――――⟶ Most of the Time

ANY COMFORT FROM HIS LOVE?

You Hardly Ever ⟵――――――――――⟶ Most of the Time
Your Church Hardly Ever ⟵――――――――――⟶ Most of the Time

ANY FELLOWSHIP TOGETHER IN THE SPIRIT?

You Hardly Ever ⟵――――――――――⟶ Most of the Time
Your Church Hardly Ever ⟵――――――――――⟶ Most of the Time

IS YOUR HEART TENDER AND COMPASSIONATE?

You Hardly Ever ⟵――――――――――⟶ Most of the Time
Your Church Hardly Ever ⟵――――――――――⟶ Most of the Time

Then make Jesus truly happy by…

agreeing wholeheartedly with each other,
loving one another,
working together with one mind and purpose.
Not being selfish,
not trying to impress others.
Being humble, thinking of others better than yourself.
Not looking out only for your own interests,
but taking an interest in others, too.
You must have the same attitude that Christ Jesus had.

Here's the explanation of Jesus and GENUINE HUMILITY. Use these words from the Bible as a prayer for Jesus-style humility:

"Though he was God, he did not think of equality with God as something to cling to. Instead, **HE GAVE UP HIS DIVINE PRIVILEGES; HE TOOK THE HUMBLE POSITION OF A SLAVE AND WAS BORN AS A HUMAN BEING. WHEN HE APPEARED IN HUMAN FORM, HE HUMBLED HIMSELF IN OBEDIENCE TO GOD AND DIED A CRIMINAL'S DEATH ON A CROSS.** Therefore, God elevated him to the place of highest honor and gave him the name above all other names, that at the name of Jesus every knee should bow, in heaven and on earth and under the earth, and every tongue confess that Jesus Christ is Lord, to the glory of God the Father.

— Philippians 2:6-11

A Travel Parable From New Guinea and Vanuatu

GENUINE HUMILITY goes both ways. Because I (Joani) have multiple sclerosis, my physical abilities are impaired. I've had to humble myself on our travels because I'm not able to balance very well or walk long distances. (But I'm not letting that stop me—it just slows me down!) I have to admit I have a disability, which is an admission of weakness that doesn't come easy for me. So that's the "humility" I must experience every day.

Here's the beauty of how God works, though: I've found that when I admit I'm weak, others jump in and complement my weakness with their strength. And that act of love touches me most when someone "strong" shows GENUINE HUMILITY.

One time, we disembarked our boat to walk into a remote New Guinea village. The villagers were ready to bedazzle us with their ornate costumes and body paint. It was a photographer's paradise! I know how much Thom loves to capture photographs, so I didn't mind bringing up the rear while he went ahead. As I hobbled along, one of the ship's photographers kindly loaned her arm to steady me. Her name is Sue Flood. Because I knew this was a once-in-a-lifetime visit to this location and she'd never been there before, I told her to go on ahead. She replied, "No, that's okay. I can help you." How sweet! I learned later that she's a famous Australian photographer honored by the Queen of England for her extraordinary work on BBC's *Planet Earth!* When a "big shot" reaches out in GENUINE HUMILITY, it's jolting. Not unlike Jesus, God's Son, who humbled himself when he joined us on this earthly journey.

145

Another example came from someone on the other end of the spectrum. On the Pacific island country of Vanuatu, we stayed in a primitive bamboo hut, eating meals in our host's small, dark hut. Each day Abraham's wife slaved away to cook for us. Over mealtime conversations, we learned our hosts were Christian. They invited us to church on Sunday. But this posed a dilemma for me because we would have to hike quite a distance through the jungle, past the grassy airstrip, and back into the jungle. But I was up for it. I'll never forget the kind, humble native woman who clutched my arm tight as we walked. "I'm sorry I'm slowing you down," I apologized. She leaned in and held my arm more tightly.

"It is my blessing," she said.

Wow! She viewed her act of serving as a blessing. Ever since, I've remembered her lesson to me. It *is* a blessing to be there for each other, to offer love through GENUINE HUMILITY.

WHY NOBODY WANTS TO GO TO CHURCH ANYMORE

How to Recognize
GENUINE HUMILITY

GENUINE HUMILITY is…

- **radically relational**. It may not make sense to anyone else when you are willing to engage someone for the sake of sharing (and being Jesus). It means meeting people on an equal plain, knowing we're all at different places on the spiritual spectrum.

What if that person were a convicted felon?

Imagine being a chaplain who loves spending time with felons known for being Ponzi-schemers, notorious gang members, drug dealers, and murderers.

Our coworker, Craig Cable, ventured behind bars to experience the radically relational ministry that Chaplain Jackman provides prisoners—criminals who've been locked up for years. Chaplain Jackman, armed with genuine humility, has created a Lifetree Café in a corrections facility where incarcerated gang members sit at tables of four, lean in, and listen to fellow inmates tell their stories in a God context. (Interesting note: Over twice as many men participate in each Lifetree Café episode as attend the traditional worship services.)

Even the prison guards marvel at what God is doing with these men. It's quite miraculous. The prisoners "staff" the conversation café, prepare publicity fliers, and serve on the Friendship Team. Their rough, tough demeanor transforms as they share in humility and honesty.

Craig told us the prisoners were stunned to think a place like Lifetree Café actually exists in the outside world. They thought Chaplain Jackman just offered the program through the Department of Corrections!

One prisoner, particularly touched by Jackman's reaching into his world, was counting down the days until his release. He told Craig he was serving his second term in prison; a third conviction would put him away for life. With an underlying sense of pleading, he shared that convicted felons like him have very few options outside of prison. Where they work, where they live, where they worship, and who they associate with has severe limitations because of the stigma that surrounds felons. He said Lifetree Café's open and accepting environment coupled with its Jesus-centered teachings are exactly what he needs when he gets out.

This man desperately wants to find a place of genuine love, grace, acceptance, and redemption. So he's looking forward to someday attending and volunteering at a Lifetree somewhere on the outside. He longs for such a place where people truly embrace that "we're all in this together."

What has Chaplain Jackman done behind bars to show Jesus? He's become a friend to prisoners, humbling himself to take a journey of faith, not sure how or if God would work. He risks showing men a new way to live in a very difficult place. That's loving with GENUINE HUMILITY.

- **open to learning from others with different beliefs.** Lifetree Café has been a testing ground for providing orthodox, biblical, Jesus-centered truth while grappling with a multitude of topics and welcoming opposing viewpoints. It works every week. To the delight and amazement of Lifetree volunteers, people of different perspectives and backgrounds walk through the doors to have spiritual conversations.

One of our favorite examples happened in Illinois when James Wysocki, the local Lifetree director, dropped off fliers at a nearby mosque several days before a program called "Muslims: What They Really Think About You." He told us, "I must say that I was more nervous about inviting Muslims to talk about Muslims than I was going into the strip clubs the month before to invite strippers to talk about strippers!"

The night of the episode, three vanloads of Muslims pulled up to engage in a conversation about faith. Christians like to talk *about* people of other religions but rarely want to talk *with* people of other religions. How can we be salt and light to those people, though, if we're never in the same room? James described the night as "Epic!" He made 23 new friends that evening all because of his GENUINE HUMILITY.

- **open to learning from people of different ages.** One of our greatest joys has been watching mixed age-levels together in Group's vacation

Bible school programs, Sunday school curriculum, Lifetree Café, overseas mission trips, and other resources and events. In today's assembly-line, age-graded mindset, we have lost the richness of learning from those of different ages. Young children bring a curiosity, freshness, and exuberance to life, while older adults offer wisdom and life experience. It's humbling to learn from a child as well as an elder.

This kind of atmosphere requires respect. In their insightful book *Training Ain't Telling*, Harold D. Stolovitch and Erica J. Keeps write, "Respect is an essential aspect of autonomy. [...] In many ways, adult learners are more fragile and vulnerable than children. The fear of failure and accompanying loss of face can be high."[1] That's why an environment filled with love is so important.

> "I tell you the truth, unless you turn from your sins and become like little children, you will never get into the Kingdom of Heaven. So **ANYONE WHO BECOMES AS HUMBLE AS THIS LITTLE CHILD IS THE GREATEST IN THE KINGDOM OF HEAVEN.**"
> — Matthew 18:3-4

> "**WISDOM BELONGS TO THE AGED**, and understanding to the old."
> — Job 12:12

149

- **admitting mistakes.** Something beautiful and wonderful happens when someone says, "I'm sorry." It's especially powerful when it's the church. *Blue Like Jazz* author Donald Miller tells a poignant story of going to a college campus to set up a confession booth…with a twist. Instead of people lining up to confess their sins, Donald's companions turned the tables and confessed the sins of the church to the people. That was a surprise.

As a church, we have our flaws, but, frankly, that's what the church is all about. We're a gathering place for the sick. And when all people—Christian or not—are honest with ourselves, we have to conclude we aren't in control. None of us. So when people say, "Christians are all a bunch of hypocrites," we need to show love with GENUINE HUMILITY and admit that, yes, we are indeed flawed.

"Jesus answered them, **HEALTHY PEOPLE DON'T NEED A DOCTOR—SICK PEOPLE DO.'** These words of Jesus were written by Luke, a doctor, in Luke 5:31. Verse 32 goes on to say, **I [JESUS] HAVE COME TO CALL NOT THOSE WHO THINK THEY ARE RIGHTEOUS, BUT THOSE WHO KNOW THEY ARE SINNERS AND NEED TO REPENT."**

— Luke 5:31-32

That's us.

- **free from churchy, insider language.** Being humble means setting aside everything that excludes others and that includes the words we use. It's easy to forget that we have our own lingo. Churches are swimming with acronyms or words that the regular person has no clue about. Words and phrases like *saved, washed in the blood,* or *Sacraments* can be completely meaningless to the uninitiated. It establishes an "us and them" mentality, not a "we're all in this together" approach.

- **putting people first.** In how many churches do custodians and building committees rule supreme? Yes, we need to be good stewards of the material gifts God has given us. But how many times do regulations take precedence over people? "No paint or tape on the walls!" "No playing on the grass!" "Only the Ladies Guild can use the kitchen!" When property is more important than ministry potential, there's a problem. One group lords it over another, and we fail to give and take with GENUINE HUMILITY.

We admit we also fell short when we moved into our new offices a few years ago. We had a policy (oh, that dreaded word!) that no one could put things on the walls or display anything above the workstation walls. Talk about a creativity killer! Plus, the policy required someone to be in charge of policing the office. We spent too much unproductive time putting property above people. We eventually abandoned our well-intentioned but Gestapo-like approach. Now when you visit our offices, you'll see an innovative environment that reflects the eclectic, unique, fun personalities of our staff. And we're more productive than ever!

- **communicating directly.** If there's one thing we've learned about working with people over the years, it's that open, clear, and straightforward communication always—*always*—makes for a healthier and happier workplace. The same is true for churches. The more we can embrace honesty and directness in our dealings with everyone in the church, the stronger our relationships will be.

Direct communication has everything to do with GENUINE HUMILITY, because it shows a pure willingness to not place yourself above others and a commitment to make sure everyone's plugged in. If there's a problem, go straight to the person who can do something about it. If you have a question, make a beeline to the person with a firsthand answer. It's transparent and, yes, can be a little messy. But that's what authentic relationships are—a bit grubby but always worth it.

151

One of Group's core values is friendliness. Here's how we describe it in our employee handbook: "We believe our work environment should be friendly, fun, fair, and forgiving. We communicate directly with one another, sharing our concerns with those who can best affect the situation. We handle our differences with love and tact, without raising our voices or lowering our integrity." Does the culture in your church follow those same principles...even with "outsiders"?

GENUINE HUMILITY is <u>not</u>...

- **Bible classes and worship that intimidate people.** No one intends this to happen, but too often we hear from people who tried a Bible class or small group and never went back. Statements like these can be very intimidating: "Open your Bible to [insert book of the Bible] and turn to chapter [insert chapter name] verse [insert verse number]. Who would like to read that aloud for the class?" *Gulp.* Put yourself in the position of someone new to church and imagine navigating this new world. Imagine coming without a Bible. Imagine trying to find a chapter and verse. Then pile on the "I can't pronounce this word" knot in your stomach. Who would want to subject themselves to this? In a world that's more and more biblically illiterate, the church must offer safe on-ramps for newbies to discover the treasures in God's Word.

- **puffed up with churchy language.** We in the church simply can't assume everyone understands what we mean. Being in the publishing business, we're especially sensitive to this and maintain a list of "red flag" words—terms from which only churched people would derive meaning. Our recent experiences with Lifetree Café have prompted us to add even more churchy words to this list as we talk with more and more people who are unfamiliar with biblical, doctrinal, and liturgical terms. GENUINE HUMILITY puts others first, so it's essential to use words they understand.

- **a place to hide.** Churches get a bad name when they hide mistakes and cover up wrongdoings. Obviously, biggies like sex scandals and financial cover-ups give churches a black eye. But even more detrimental are rumors and parking lot whisperings. Too many meetings have ended with a smaller group huddling outside the building to complain about what really went on in the meeting. Or people gossiping because they can't bring themselves to speak directly to the person they have an issue with. There's absolutely nothing humble about that. Transparency and truth-telling are hard. But they're necessary if we're to love with GENUINE HUMILITY.

- **property obsessed.** If you want to know what's important to a church, read its newsletter or attend its leadership meetings. Churches in decline focus on paving the parking lot, repairing the roof, and how the youth group messed up the fellowship hall. Whether lives are being changed through their ministry efforts doesn't seem to come up much.

- **a clique or club.** Yes, we share a common bond in Christ, and we love being with those who are "like us." But Christians have a reputation for huddling in cliques, a tendency that can permeate virtually any church, large or small. Recently, a public school teacher who works with underprivileged children overheard a child say, "My dad says churches are for rich people, 'cause they're always asking for money. We can't afford to go to church." Ouch! That smacks more of a country club than the body of Christ.

- **sheep stealing and competitive.** Pastors and church leaders want to do their best for the Lord, but frankly, pastor conferences and youth ministry events can become a prideful breeding ground for bragging and comparisons. And sad to say, most church growth today comes from disgruntled Christians moving from one church to another, not from an influx of new believers.

At a recent Simply Youth Ministry Conference, we established some ground rules right up front for the 2,800 youth workers in attendance. The one that got the biggest applause? "No numbers. Attendance, budgets, salaries—all are off limits." The sigh of relief around the room could have lifted a hot-air balloon!

Understanding GENUINE HUMILITY is one thing. Infusing it into every aspect of your church culture is another. The next chapter will give you specific strategies for making that happen.

153

Endnote

1. Harold D. Stolovitch and Erica J. Keeps, *Telling Ain't Training* (Alexandria, VA: American Society for Training and Development, 2002), 51.

10 PRACTICAL WAYS TO LOVE WITH GENUINE HUMILITY

To be genuinely humble, we must BE LIKE JESUS.

If you ask the people in your church (and yourself, for that matter) if they believe they're humble, most of them will readily say yes (it's the "right" answer). But if you ask them if they actually practice GENUINE HUMILITY on a regular basis—and provide some specific examples—the answers might not be as positive.

Are they (and you) "radically relational"? Are they (and you) open to learning from others of different beliefs? Are they (and you) open to learning from others of different ages (even those who are younger)? Do they (and you) consistently admit mistakes? Do they (and you) value people above buildings and rules? Do they (and you) always communicate directly?

If you don't get an overwhelming "yes!" to all these questions, then your church needs some improvement. This chapter offers specific, practical tips for loving others with GENUINE HUMILITY.

(The first step is simple: Just be humble enough to admit that you can do better!)

BE INTENTIONAL
About Relationships

To be GENUINELY HUMBLE, we must be like Jesus. We embody what God wants the world to see—a relational, incarnational ministry. We reach out to others as Jesus did. More than ever, our culture today is crying out for leaders and churches who value face-to-face, voice-to-voice, heart-to-heart interaction. Sadly, our society is losing the ability to deal with others in a healthy way. Instead of loving others, our time devolves into competing, complaining, fighting, hiding, avoiding, bullying, shouting, and worse. People have forgotten how to communicate effectively.

Your church can offer opportunities for people to practice relational skills. Wouldn't it be amazing if your church had a reputation that prompted people to say, "If you want friends who really care about you, you can always count on [insert your church name here]"?

43%
DISCUSS IMPORTANT MATTERS WITH NO ONE OR ONLY ONE OTHER PERSON

"The number of people saying there is no one with whom they discussed important matters nearly tripled in 20 years."

Sociologists are shocked at what's happening in our culture. Researchers found "the number of people saying there is no one with whom they discussed important matters nearly tripled" in 20 years. And "almost half of the population (43.6 percent) now [report] that they discuss important matters with either no one or with only one other person." The largest loss of discussion partners or relationships comes from a decrease in ties binding us to community and neighborhood.[1]

156

> For all its industrial efficiency and scalability, its transhemispheric reach and its grand civil integrity, Facebook is still a painfully blunt instrument for doing the delicate work of transmitting human relationships. It's an excellent utility for sending and receiving data, but we are not data, and relationships cannot be reduced to the exchange of information or making binary decisions between liking and not liking, friending and unfriending.[2]

FOR THOSE WHO EXALT THEMSELVES WILL BE HUMBLED, AND THOSE WHO HUMBLE THEMSELVES WILL BE EXALTED.
— Luke 14:11

Read the entire account of Jesus' teaching about humility in Luke 14:7-14. What does this mean for our churches today?

BE INTENTIONALLY
With Others

Be fully present.

In their book *Click,* authors Ori and Rom Brafman talk about three key components of being present. They describe what one doctor learned about the first component, *intentionality:* "She needed to become present so that the patient felt seen and understood. [...Intentionality] means entering an interaction with a sense of purpose and conscious awareness. Intentionality means giving the interaction our undivided attention, instead of going through the motions of being preoccupied with other things."[3]

The second component is *mutuality:* being open and available to meet others where they are. Mutuality means focusing on the shared aspects of

157

trust and honesty involved in a relationship, rather than giving advice or trying to solve problems.

The third is what the Brafman brothers call *resonance:* "Resonance doesn't just make us feel more connected to our surroundings; research shows that at its core, resonance is contagious. We tend to match the emotions of those around us."[4]

Simply put, your loving presence is contagious. Remember, you're modeling Jesus to people. Jesus' love is contagious, and others can experience it through you.

Our friend Deb shared with us a great example of GENUINE HUMILITY from her home church. Every year Flatirons Community Church hosts an over-the-top event called "Shine: The Big Party." It honors those who have been marginalized by society—those who were never invited to a prom or other popular shindig, such as young people with mental challenges or those with Down syndrome. They call it a time when the "proud get humbled and the humbled get elevated," and everyone involved agrees that nothing equals the experience of witnessing so much joy in others. "Being a part of this is what the heart of God looks like. It teaches true compassion; moving someone else's pain from your head to your heart to your hands," Deb told us.

The relationships between the church volunteers and attendees don't always end when the party is over. Deb has seen many of them meeting in the church lobby and sometimes sitting with their Shine escorts at church services. She said, "It's made our community tighter in many ways. For so long our growing church was looked on as a source of traffic snarls and long lines at Starbucks on the weekends. Now more people are checking the church out. Some are even bumping into Jesus in the process."

STOP Competing

The world is watching. When churches compete with other churches, "sheep steal," and guard their turf, people are put off. The unchurched are already confused by all the denominations and bickering over theology. *They* think the church should be about Jesus—and wasn't he the guy who preached love?

158

Churches *can* work together! The most exciting and surprising thing has happened over the years with our vacation Bible school materials. In the early years, churches would say they couldn't use Group's VBS because the church across the street or town was using it. That was competitive thinking. Over time we watched a transformation take place. Instead of going head to head, churches now work together. VBS directors attend Group's VBS networking parties called "FunShops: Training with a Twist." Each year these local gatherings allow those who care about kids to network and learn from one another. It's a big win for everyone; churches now work together to build and share fun-themed sets. Instead of competing, children's ministry leaders are now cooperating. Together, they're beacons of light.

Beware of
"PROFESSIONALS"

There's no such thing as a "humility pro."

We often say our experience can be our worst enemy—especially when it comes to claiming your own expertise. We must embrace lifelong learning and not forget that those we're "teaching" don't have our life experiences and understanding.

> Most experts are so familiar with their topic that they forget what it is like to be a novice. Even if they remember, experts can become bored with having to repeat the fundamentals over and over again.[5]
> — John J. Medina, *Brain Rules*

> So where does this leave the philosophers, the scholars, and the world's brilliant debaters?...

159

God has made the wisdom of this world look foolish... **I DIDN'T USE LOFTY WORDS OR IMPRESSIVE WISDOM** to tell you God's secret plan. For I decided...I would forget everything except Jesus Christ, the one who was crucified.

— 1 Corinthians 1:20; 2:1-2

What Did They Do Before the Bible?

It occurred to me that the first people who heard or read the Bible didn't need a dictionary or a concordance. When Isaiah preached, the people didn't have to organize a seminar and hire a professor to figure out what he said. When Mark's Gospel showed up in a community, they didn't feel the necessity of putting together a six-month study course on Wednesday evenings. All these books came out of the common life and common knowledge of the people, many, maybe even most, of them illiterate. Not unintelligent, mind you, but not schooled. So why was I intruding all my knowledge *about* the Bible into their reading of it?[6]

— Eugene H. Peterson, *Eat This Book*

The great cruelty is that the smarter you get about something, the harder it is to share what you know.[7]

— Dan Heath, *Made to Stick*

INTENTIONALLY LEARN FROM
Those Who Are Different From You

Rubbing shoulders with people you don't normally associate with can truly change your life. That's one of the reasons we love to travel to other cultures. It forces us out of our comfort zones—sometimes *way* out of our comfort zones. But it's a powerful way to keep us humble.

In the past, we'd take our youth groups to visit other churches and other religions. Not only was it an interesting experience, it also strengthened our own kids' faith. Our Group Workcamps and Week of Hope experiences bring youth groups of various Christian traditions together. Some fear this might weaken kids' faith, but it typically has the opposite result. In fact, leaders often tell us this may be one of the biggest benefits of the camps. Kids have respectful conversations with those from different traditions. Teenagers and adults learn more about their own tradition's beliefs and often come away with stronger faith because they've genuinely grappled with it.

Let's pause and take a close look at some specific examples. What do the following interactions tell you about GENUINE HUMILITY? How would you react if these people walked through your church doors?

- **A Transgender**
  One of our Lifetree Café branches welcomed a transgender man and his wife. The man said he was so impressed with the people at Lifetree that he was thinking of attending the branch's sponsoring church, which he never would have thought possible before attending Lifetree.

- **A Witch**
  Here's the response from a woman who attended a Lifetree episode on Wicca, paganism, and Christianity called "The Witch Next Door":

  "Thank you for your interest in me. […] I am the witch next door. There are many like me. I live in a nice neighborhood about five minutes from your church. I am married with two children, a master's degree, and a fulltime job; I pay taxes and I vote. I have morals and values.

161

"The appeal of Wicca and paganism is this: It's simply another way of finding spiritual fulfillment that resonates as strongly and profoundly in me as Christianity does in you. [...] We've been criticized, misunderstood, teased, persecuted, and far worse throughout the ages, all in the name of Jesus Christ who said, 'Do unto others as you would have them do unto you.'

"This is what I am asking here. Treat us as you would like us to treat you."

Embrace People of
ALL AGES

Our culture is obsessed with segregating people into age groups. But God designed all of us to regularly connect with people of all ages. Children often play with kids who are older or younger than they are, and, of course, families are made up of people of all ages. Combining ages creates a dynamic environment for faith to grow. We've seen this with millions of kids and youth in Group's vacation Bible school programs and Workcamps, which regularly demonstrate the beauty of people of all ages working, playing, and discovering Jesus together.

When considering mixing age groups, some people worry about discipline problems, while others worry that kids won't be responsible or positive. They rack up a whole list of potential problems. But we've learned that mingling ages actually strengthens relationships *and* faith. It's a mystery to us why parents and leaders don't embrace this concept. It really, really works!

I (Joani) remember a particular meeting with the children's ministry team at our church. We were discussing a midweek curriculum that uses the concept of multi-age small groups. One parent said, "My daughter wouldn't want to be with a younger child." Another parent chimed in, "My daughter wouldn't like that either!" I watched what happens all too often in meetings. A well-founded, tested, proven concept is dismissed by people who've had no experience with it.

I spent my grade school years in a one-room country schoolhouse with 12 other students, only one of whom was in my "grade." From kindergarten through eighth grade, I experienced the power of multi-age groupings. I still remember an "upperclassman" taking me by the hand and helping me find the outdoor restroom. I eavesdropped on older kids' lessons and mentored the little kids as I grew older. Children naturally assumed leadership roles and worked out their differences on their own.

Some schools are rediscovering this and are pairing older kids with younger kids as reading buddies. Kids love that! It's a normal, natural part of life when the young and old learn from each other.

(Then there's the controversy of having children in worship with their parents…but that's another book.)

We've also seen the benefits of multi-age groups in Lifetree Café. Here's a story from a Lifetree Café in Iowa:

Five 8- to 10-year-old boys attended an episode called "Confronting Bullies." At one point, everyone in the room was asked to brainstorm ideas for dealing with bullies. One of the boys stood up and eloquently and compassionately listed his group's ideas. The adults in the room were amazed. Where else could a 10-year-old have a voice—an equal voice—in such an important issue?

But that isn't the end of the story. Later that evening, the mom who had brought three of the boys called the director of the Lifetree branch and described how this event had sparked a desire among all of the boys to make a difference. That week, they noticed that the equipment in their neighborhood park was unsafe, so they started a petition, got all the neighborhood kids to sign it, and sent it off to the city officials. Within days they received a letter from the city thanking them and promising to make the necessary repairs.

> "But we have this treasure in jars of clay to show that this **ALL-SURPASSING POWER IS FROM GOD AND NOT FROM US.**"
>
> — 2 Corinthians 4:7

PRACTICAL WAYS TO LOVE WITH **GENUINE HUMILITY**

Model **VULNERABILITY**

When leaders model vulnerability by sharing a slice of their own lives, others are moved to do the same. One of our friends in children's ministry shared with us about a teacher who told the kids in her Sunday school class, "This morning I had a fight with my husband." The kids gasped; they weren't used to this kind of transparency in church. She said, "I didn't like that I was impatient. I needed God to help me." Through her willingness to be authentic, these children realized how God can make a real difference in the life of a real person.

It's all about living in the truth. We in the church have tried so hard for so long to show the world that we have it all together. What a relief to finally admit that no one has it all together this side of heaven!

In every episode of Lifetree Café, the host models vulnerability by sharing a story from his or her own life that connects with the topic at hand. This kind of authentic sharing opens the heart of everyone else in the room and gives each person permission to share at a deep, vulnerable level.

During the first few years of developing the Lifetree concept, we didn't do this. But since adding this ingredient, relationships have strengthened and deepened much faster.

We can't expect others to go where we ourselves aren't willing to go.

Here's a great question for church leaders: Are you willing to share how your faith intersects with your questions and struggles? Your flock will follow your lead.

> Our natural desire to reciprocate by being vulnerable—and consequently take the relationship to a deeper level—is so ingrained in us that scientists have found it can even be triggered by a desktop computer.[8]
>
> — Ori and Rom Brafman, *Click*

> When facts become so widely available and instantly accessible, each one becomes less valuable. What begins to matter more is the ability to place these facts in *context* and to deliver them with *emotional impact.*[9]
> — Daniel H. Pink, *A Whole New Mind*

DO: Experience a foot washing. Read about Jesus washing the disciples' feet in John 13. Some churches incorporate this ancient practice. Most don't. We urge you to take a risk and try it.

We've done this with large groups by asking everyone to take off their shoes. You can imagine the uncomfortable murmurs and occasional protests. But that's okay. We choose a few people's feet to wash and dry, and the crowd is usually riveted. Next, we ask people to pair up and tell a partner what they felt during that experience—regardless of whether theirs were the feet that were washed. Then we dig deeper. We ask how their emotions were like or unlike those the disciples might have experienced. We have pairs report their discoveries to the group at large.

Next Sunday, have the pastor carry a basin and a towel and kneel to wash the feet of a few people. Do this as a worship experience or a deeper learning experience. Be prepared for powerful discoveries about servanthood and humility.

Cut the **COMMITTEES**

We can't think of anyone who ever said, "I just *love* being in committee meetings!" Committees foster indecision, stifle creativity, drain emotions, breed conflict, generate distrust, and kill action. It's no wonder they have a bad reputation.

Let people loose! Encourage others to serve. Don't scare them off with hundreds of hoops to jump through. Although organizations do, by definition, need to be organized, longstanding committees, boards, councils, and bureaucracies broadcast the message that we're really *not* all in this together. In fact, people who like and need power tend to rule committees, which is the antithesis of GENUINE HUMILITY.

Conduct a
"RULES AUDIT"

Walk through your church and look for signs. Are they people-friendly or property-friendly? Do your signs protect your building or do they promote relationships? Do your signs shout "No!" and "Off limits!" or do they encourage unlimited interaction?

This simple step is one of the easiest and most practical ways you can promote GENUINE HUMILITY in your church.

Endnotes

1. Miller McPherson, Lynn Smith-Lovin, and Matthew E. Brashears, "Social Isolation in America: Changes in Core Discussion Networks over Two Decades," American Sociological Review, Vol. 71 (2006): 353.

2. Lev Grossman, "2010 Person of the Year: Mark Zuckerberg," Time, December 27, 2010/January 3, 2011, 72.

3. Ori Brafman and Rom Brafman, Click (New York, NY: Broadway Books, 2010), 88.

4. Ibid., 90.

5. John J. Medina, Brain Rules: 12 Principles for Surviving and Thriving at Work, Home, and School (Seattle, WA: Pear Press, 2008), 88.

6. Eugene H. Peterson, Eat This Book (Grand Rapids, MI: Eerdmans Publishing, 2006), 166.

7. Mike Hofman, "Chip and Dan Heath: Marketing Made Sticky," Inc. Magazine, January 1, 2007, http://www.inc.com/magazine/20070101/salesmarketing-campaigns.html.

8. Ori Brafman and Rom Brafman, Click (New York, NY: Broadway Books, 2010), 45.

9. Daniel H. Pink, A Whole New Mind (New York, NY: Berkley Publishing, 2006), 103.

11

ACT OF LOVE #4
DIVINE
ANTICIPATION

Probably the most POWERFUL AND MYSTERIOUS ACT OF LOVE IS DIVINE ANTICIPATION.

We can't fully understand or explain in human terms what happens when it happens. But it does!

DIVINE ANTICIPATION isn't a freaky, weird way to live. It's actually quite natural for us to tune into the supernatural. Let's start with a story about a Lifetree Café episode called "Is God Real? An Ethiopian Prime Minister's Encounter With God."

The episode revolved around a thought-provoking and amazing interview with Tamrat Layne, a controversial communist leader who did lots of horrible things in his African country when he was in power. He was arrested and imprisoned, and it was during his time in prison that he claims he had an encounter with Jesus.

Really.

It's one thing to preach about the reality of God's existence. It's another to discuss and argue about it. But it's an entirely different thing to *experience* it. So that's what we did. We talked about the veracity of Tamrat's story. Then we said, "Let's give it a try."

Here are the actual instructions we gave the group:

I'd like you to join me in an experience—one in which we ask God to show up. Not in a bright light—though that would be memorable! I'm thinking of something more personal and, possibly, far more powerful.

Please find a partner—preferably someone you don't know well. Feel free to move your chairs so you and your partner can talk easily. Once you've found a partner, briefly introduce yourself. (Pause.) Thank you.

Shortly, I'll ask you to do something you might find uncomfortable. I'll ask you to close your eyes and think about your partner. And while you're doing that, I'll ask you to listen. God may have a message for your partner.

This isn't a parlor game or some sort of trick. And to do this you don't necessarily have to believe in God or Jesus. Paul didn't believe in Jesus, but Paul still heard from him. Ditto for Tamrat.

We're simply asking God a question and listening—for just 60 seconds— for a response. That response might come in the form of a mental picture...a phrase...a Scripture reference...anything. Whatever it is, don't resist it. A mental image of a bicycle might not mean anything to you, but it might be very meaningful to your partner.

Maybe you'll hear something God wants to pass along to your partner, and maybe you won't. That's okay, too. But we won't know unless we create a space where we're actually listening.

If you believe God is real, here's a chance to connect with him. If you don't believe God is real, here's a chance to think about someone else for 60 seconds, and that's a good thing, too.

Willing to give this a go?

The question I'd like you to ask God is this: What does my partner need today?

Don't try to figure it out from something your partner said or how your partner looks. This isn't the time to tell your partner he needs a haircut and blame it on God.

Instead, just ask God the question, and see what—if anything—comes to mind.

I'll begin with a brief prayer to set this up, and then you simply ask that question and listen. Let's just see how this goes. (Pause.)

Dear God, please silence all those voices that fill our heads.

Silence our own thoughts and voices for the next 60 seconds.

Silence the voices that come from anywhere other than you.

We're listening, God.

What does our partner need today? (Wait 60 seconds, and then say:)

Amen.

Now let's check in with our partners.

But before we do, let me tell you this: It's up to you to decide if what your partner shares is from God or maybe the result of a bad burrito. If your partner shares something that resonates with you, if your heart just embraces it, then receive it. If not, nod kindly, and accept our thanks for trying this.

Do this with your partner: Share what—if anything—came to mind regarding your partner. (Allow time for people to share.)

Thanks for giving that experience a try. If you heard from God concerning your partner, great. If not, that's okay, too. What matters most is that you were listening.

You know what happened? God showed up in miraculous ways. Ways that rocked people's world.

We didn't know what might happen. But we took a risk, and that risk changed people's lives in astounding ways. Here is just a small sampling of the stories we heard after the episode:

- During "listening" time, Shawna saw concentric circles, hearts, and a stuffed giraffe. When she described what she saw, her partner started crying. She was attending a three-day conference and was far from home. This was her first time away from her 4-year-old daughter, and she was missing her intensely. Her daughter's favorite toy was a stuffed giraffe.

- Matt saw a big meadow and an oak tree with a rope swing. Next to it, he saw a garden. At first, Matt wanted to dismiss it as a screensaver image. When he reluctantly shared what he'd seen, his partner, Aaron, was visibly moved. His father had recently died, and the family had just finished his memorial by planting an oak tree in his honor. They'd scattered his ashes in a big open space on his property in Texas. Aaron reached for his phone and showed Matt pictures. There was a structure there and a rope swing on the other side of the house, which was his dad's escape. His dad's favorite pastime was gardening. Aaron felt that the picture that came to Matt's mind was one way God found to comfort him during his difficult transition.

- Ali wrote down her experience: "Tonight, the topic at Lifetree Café was 'Is God Real?' After a video about a man who encountered Jesus in a vision, we were encouraged to find a partner—someone we didn't know well—and then close our eyes for a minute and listen to God to see if he had a message for that person. I have to admit, a part of me was a little skeptical. It felt a little bit like calling Ms. Cleo for my free reading. Somehow I have no trouble believing that God spoke to Old Testament prophets, but I have trouble believing that he speaks to us today.

"But I did it, and all I could picture was an hourglass. I thought, 'This is probably just because we're supposed to do this for a minute, and my brain is counting down the time.' Even so, I told my partner what had come to my mind, and she knew exactly what God was telling her. She's supposed to have a heart valve replacement in a few years, and she's worried about how it will go. She'd been telling her husband she felt like time was running out and she hadn't done everything she wanted to do with her life.

"Then she shared what God had told her for me. 'I feel like God's saying you really love what you do for work, but you want to do more with your life.' That's when I started to think there was something to this whole thing. It was just what I'd blogged about a couple of weeks ago, about dreams and about wanting to write more. It perfectly captured the things I've been feeling. I told her so. I told her that I do love my job, but work has been so stressful and overwhelming lately that I've been too exhausted to pursue my writing. When we said goodbye a bit later, she said, 'I feel like God wants me to give you this word: *Seek*. Seek, seek, seek. He'll do what you want to happen. Maybe not in the way you expect, but he'll use you. Seek.' There's still a part of me that finds this whole thing a little odd. But, hey, seeking God is biblical. So that's what I'm going to do."

- Candace's partner saw the letter V, the first letter of Candace's mother's name. Candace had recently sinned against her mother and then conveniently forgot about it. This felt like the Holy Spirit knocking her on the head to confess to her mother and ask for forgiveness.

- Two years ago, we met Giovy when she attended a Lifetree Café training. We remember her because she was probably the most skeptical Lifetree trainee we'd ever met. She sat in the back of the room, arms crossed, challenging the premise of Lifetree at every turn.

  But what happened next changed her life. It began during the same episode, "Is God Real?" She paired up with someone she didn't know who happened to be a pastor's wife. The group was given the same instructions, and she thought, "I'm supposed to listen for some spiritual thing for the pastor's wife, so throughout the 60 seconds, I'm thinking, 'Okay God, give me something good because here's this pastor's wife and she's a spiritual person.'" The only thing that came to mind was an image of bamboo. And she thought, "Come on God; give me something." But the idea in her mind didn't change; it was still bamboo. She thought, "This is the weirdest thing."

When the minute was over, her partner told Giovy what God had shown her for Giovy. It was a beautiful spiritual thing. Then the pastor's wife asked, "What did God show you for me?" Giovy replied, "I don't even want to say. I'm really embarrassed…all I saw was… bamboo." The pastor's wife sat back in her chair, the color draining from her face, her eyes tearing up. Giovy thought, "What did I say?" The woman then said, "Two weeks ago I was reading a devotional about the bamboo tree and how it's a strong tree but also flexible. I feel that I need to be more flexible, and that devotion pointed out the thing that I need to work on. I'm working on it; God is working on me. That devotional has been in my head for the last two weeks. And now you say the word *bamboo*." They were both thinking, "Wow! This is incredible! Only God can do this!"

A few weeks later, Giovy received a package at home that had "LIVE" written on it. Inside was a bamboo shoot.

Giovy told us, "I have grown more in the last two years through Lifetree than in 43 years of my Christian walk. I now realize I've been pushing people away. I realize that faith is a process. I'm a changed person."

She truly is a different person than she was two years ago—and the bamboo shoot the pastor's wife sent her is now two feet tall.

The Lifetree Café experiment has required us to trust in the Holy Spirit completely…and to hand over control to God.

But God's involvement isn't always immediately apparent. Here's another story of DIVINE ANTICIPATION:

Shawna and the Lifetree video team were looking for some video editing help, so they reached out to the community to see if anyone was interested. They received a résumé from a young man who loved Group and had been to Lifetree Café before. He seemed promising, so they brought him in for a lunch meeting to talk about his work.

When he walked in the front doors of Group, he looked really familiar to Shawna. She couldn't place him, but he immediately recognized her. "I know you!" he said.

He remembered that he and his wife had sat with Shawna at Lifetree Café more than a year ago.

His wife had inadvertently discovered that her little brother had been involved in a homosexual relationship. She was extremely surprised and told her husband. Two days later, they saw an ad in the paper for the Lifetree program "My Son Is Gay: When Faith and Sexual Orientation Collide." They decided to attend and try to figure out how to talk to her brother.

Shawna remembered that they'd had a great talk during the program, discovering together the importance of loving people, regardless of whether we endorse their behavior. The couple even brought their parents to the next showing two days later.

Over lunch, Shawna got an update on how all of that was going. At the end of the meal, he looked down at his hands and said, "I just have to tell you this because I want you to know what Lifetree is doing in our lives, even though we've only come to three episodes. I was late for our lunch because we were meeting with a detective."

Intrigued, Shawna asked him to explain what Lifetree had to do with a detective.

After attending the program about homosexuality and faith, his wife attended an episode called "Breaking the Cycle of Sexual Abuse" and brought a friend who was struggling with this issue. His wife didn't realize what the program would stir up in her own life. When she was in high school, she'd been sexually abused by a female youth worker and had never talked about it until this program.

As a result, she and her husband decided to report the incident, because their biggest fear was that this youth worker had abused others. As the police dug into the incident, four other girls (her high school friends) came forward and said that they, too, had been abused. It was uncomfortable and scary, but they decided to move forward with an investigation after hearing that this wasn't an isolated incident.

That morning, he and his wife had been meeting with a detective and had called to confront this youth worker. At the end of the phone call, the youth worker apologized for hurting her. It wasn't a confession, but it was what they needed to move forward with a full-fledged investigation.

The video editor ended his story and pointed to Lifetree's calendar of topics. He said that Lifetree Café had changed his life and pushed him and his family into uncomfortable situations that would have been easier to ignore—but the healing had been worth it. "You have to know," he said, "how much people's lives are being changed by Lifetree. Don't stop, okay?"

Living in DIVINE ANTICIPATION means trusting God even when it's scary and unpredictable.

What's So Compelling About **DIVINE ANTICIPATION?**

DIVINE ANTICIPATION is living in the mystery and wonder of God. More than ever, our culture has squeezed our understanding of life into measurable facts, figures, analyses, scientific findings, technology, and cold, hard proof. Yet God still manages to overtake us. We can't make the sun shine or the rain fall. We can't bring a body to life, and we can't explain how the world came to be and how it keeps spinning. From the incomprehensible, overwhelming nature of the universe to the tiniest forms of life, our world is full of mystery. And the mystery is most profound when it's played out in every stage of our lives—birth, death, relationships, achievement, loss, joy, sorrow, questions, and answers.

That said, DIVINE ANTICIPATION means we emphasize God's reality, presence, and action in our lives today. Life is amazing, incredible, and wonderful *now!* The church has done a great job of emphasizing God's might throughout history; all those Sunday school classes and Bible courses point us to the God of history in Bible times. We need to remember every day, every hour that God is as awesome today as ever.

We're calling for a movement that not only celebrates the acts of God recorded in the Bible but equally emphasizes what God is doing today. DIVINE ANTICIPATION invites and trains people to watch for God in action today. To live with the understanding that "God is here, ready to connect with you in a fresh way" is utterly transformative.

> So the Word became human and made his home among us. **HE WAS FULL OF UNFAILING LOVE AND FAITHFULNESS.** And we have seen his glory, the glory of the Father's one and only son.
>
> — John 1:14

173

Jesus-Style **DIVINE ANTICIPATION**

Jesus lived a life of DIVINE ANTICIPATION. His whole purpose fulfilled God's will.

God's Son also gave us clues for how to live in DIVINE ANTICIPATION. Perhaps the time in Jesus' life when he may have been most anticipatory was just before his crucifixion. What did it mean for him to live totally connected to God the Father?

Put yourself in this scene. You've just experienced a foot washing and a meal of bread and wine. Jesus gave new meaning to the food and drink. Then Jesus said something about someone betraying him. Craziness. Everything is madly swirling around in your head and heart. What's going on? Nothing makes sense. What's happening? Then…

"As soon as Judas left the room, Jesus said, 'The time has come for the Son of Man to enter into his glory, and God will be glorified because of him. And since God receives glory because of the Son, he will soon give glory to the Son. […] So now I am giving you a new commandment: *Love each other. Just as I have loved you, you should love each other. Your love for one another will prove to the world that you are my disciples'*" (John 13:31-35).

In this unsettling time, Jesus pointed to love. And God's ultimate act of love was about to unfold upon a cross.

The Ultimate **DIVINE ANTICIPATION**

Jesus paved the way for us. He showed us how to glorify God through love. What a brilliant plan! Instead of hard, unmovable stone temples, God designed people—*us*—to be his living temples, pointing others to God by loving them.

The rest is history. His story plus our story. A love story.

As we, the church, strive to live out our calling, maybe, just maybe, we can love more deeply. Because of Jesus.

As we said earlier, we've reenacted the foot washing experience with thousands of people over the years. One was especially memorable. We were with a large group in Cuba. I (Thom) knelt down with a basin of water, gently washing people's feet while Joani followed with a soft towel. We looked people in the eye as we washed and dried their feet.

We were planning to use this experience to demonstrate how God taps into emotions to draw his people closer to him. Unexpectedly, someone stood up and said, "We want to wash *your* feet." The entire group broke into spontaneous worship, honoring the presence of Christ among us. We abandoned the rest of our lesson plan and basked in the Holy Spirit's presence.

Later, we talked about what had happened that night in an impoverished, suppressed, government-controlled culture. We had experienced the pure power of Jesus. We had led the foot washing experience many times, but nothing like that had ever happened before. Our host explained, "Don't you realize what it meant to these people that you—the American teachers, authors, leaders, the people they esteem—would kneel down and wash their feet?" No, we hadn't. God used us to be Jesus to them—and vice versa.

In Cuba, the grip of communism is palpable. "Give us our daily bread" isn't a trite, symbolic prayer. It's a literal request. The bakery shelves are often bare. People line up every day for rations of food. Simple things like toothpaste can be unavailable for extended periods of time.

Unlike some other communist regimes, though, Cuba tolerates the church. And God's people in Cuba have a special glow. We in the American church can learn some things from them.

When we returned to our own church, we found ourselves making comparisons. Here at home the amplified sounds of our worship band and polished singers overpower the sanctuary. In contrast, the voices of the Cuban congregations fill the room.

Worship in the American church has become largely a professional stage performance. Worship in the Cuban church is genuinely participatory. Cubans sing and worship with gusto. In our country, we pay the professionals to worship for us.

The Cuban church's approach to growth also struck us. Churches start in people's homes. They can accommodate as many people as fit in a living room or backyard. "Then what?" we asked. "Does the church move to a larger building?" No. The government won't authorize new church facilities. So when one home church fills, they simply start another one in a different home with new leaders.

For them, the goal is not a crowd. Nor do they focus on a gifted communicator. They focus on Christ and his body.

We love our country and the freedoms we enjoy. But we marvel at the faithfulness of God's people who exude freedom—not in the state—but in the Lord.

How can we do that?

Be Open to
FRESH WAYS OF
ENCOUNTERING GOD

Trust the Holy Spirit.

Barna studies indicate that only 44 percent of people say they experience God on a typical Sunday morning.[1] That's discouraging. However, 83 percent who attend Lifetree Café say they experience God, and 95 percent say they grow closer with others.[2] That's extremely encouraging!

But here's something that may surprise you.

When some pastors and churched people attend Lifetree Café for the first time, they say something different. Pastors and church staff often rate the experience very differently from regular people. We believe it's because they have a narrow view of what it means to experience God. They're people who are reached through traditional, passive sermon listening. Of course, God can work in that situation. But God works in other ways, as well. That might surprise us, but it shouldn't. The Bible is full of examples of God working in astounding, unexpected ways.

We love what Francis Chan has to say about allowing the Holy Spirit to work. "From my perspective, the Holy Spirit is tragically neglected and, for all practical purposes, forgotten. While no evangelical would deny His existence, I'm willing to believe there are millions of churchgoers across America who cannot confidently say they have experienced His presence or action in their lives over the past year. And many of them do not believe they can," writes Chan in his book *Forgotten God.*[3]

Regular churchgoers may not believe they can experience God, but hundreds of non-churchgoers sure want to. For Chan, this realization was born out of something very personal. He says, "There was a time when I got excited over a crowd showing up to hear me preach, but those days are long gone. Now I deeply desire that the Spirit of God would do things that I *know* are not of me and that cannot be faked or accounted for by human reason."[4]

He goes on to explain the profound implications of ignoring the power of the Holy Spirit in church ministry:

> If I were Satan and my ultimate goal was to thwart God's kingdom and purposes, one of my main strategies would be to get churchgoers to ignore the Holy Spirit. The degree to which this has happened (and I would argue that it is a prolific disease in the body of Christ) is directly connected to the dissatisfaction most of us feel with and in the church. We understand something very important is missing. The feeling is so strong that some have run away from the church and God's Word completely.
>
> I believe that this missing *something* is actually a missing *Someone*—namely, the Holy Spirit. Without Him, people operate in their own strength and only accomplish human-size results. The world is not moved by love or actions that are of human creation. And the church is not empowered to live differently from any other gathering of people without the Holy Spirit. But when believers live in the power of the Spirit, the evidence in their lives is supernatural. The church cannot help but be different, and the world cannot help but notice.[5]

We completely agree with Francis Chan—the "world cannot help but notice" when we let the Spirit take control of our faith, especially when it comes to our experience at church.

DIVINE ANTICIPATION is all about letting God work. So how do we know when we see it?

How to Recognize DIVINE ANTICIPATION

DIVINE ANTICIPATION is...

- **realizing God is actively involved—all the time.** Like radio waves, God is there; we just need to tune in. We expectantly trust, believe, hope, and know God is at work.

  God is alive today. We see him in our daily decisions, nature, a newborn baby, or an act of kindness. God is all around us. God is alive and real. He is…active. here. now. But most people don't know for sure that he's really here. Not that they don't know about Jesus. They just think he's dead.

Eugene Peterson expresses it beautifully in *Eat This Book*:

> [God] is present, often unnoticed, frequently anonymous, among actual men and women located in time and place, in the context of their ancestors and in the towns and valleys and mountains in which they had all grown up. And there's a lot more stories of the same sort. These are the stories that formed Israel's imagination—quiet, everyday, the supernatural camouflaged in the natural, the presence of God revealed in the places and among the people involved in our day to day living.[6]

God *is* real. It's just that people have forgotten to notice.

For years—in our Workcamp program with teenagers, in our vacation Bible school programs, and in our Sunday school curriculum—we have challenged people to look for what God is doing, to look for "God Sightings."

People have told us about tens of thousands of God Sightings. One youth group that attended a Week of Hope (a Group mission trip) had a great experience at the camp and reported God Sightings every day. But it wasn't until *after* the camp when their bus broke down that they became aware of God's moment-by-moment protective hand. While traveling on Trail Ridge Road in Rocky Mountain National Park, the highest continuous road in the United States, their bus' brakes went out, and fire and smoke began billowing around the bus. Miraculously, the driver was able to stop the bus, and everyone walked away uninjured. Not only did God keep the youth group safe from near disaster, but passersby also helped the group procure vans to shuttle them safely down the mountain and take them home. The youth group couldn't wait to tell us about their continued God Sightings even after the mission trip was over. When we imagine how God can use every daily experience to draw us closer to him, it totally changes our perspective.

Wouldn't it be amazing if the people in your community experienced God Sightings every week at your church? That's DIVINE ANTICIPATION.

- **grasping God's power.** We need to fully understand that the power that brought Jesus back from the dead is the same power working in and through us. That's supernatural power! We echo Paul's prayer: "I also pray that you will understand the incredible greatness of God's power for us who believe him. This is the same mighty power that raised Christ from the dead and seated him in the place of honor at God's right hand in the heavenly realms" (Ephesians 1:19-20).

Putting the 4 ACTS OF LOVE into practice is possible when we trust that God is working through us every day, just as he promised.

Dive into those words! What incredible God-adventure awaits you? Do you believe this enough to take the plunge?

> I tell you the truth, **ANYONE WHO BELIEVES IN ME WILL DO THE SAME WORKS I HAVE DONE, AND EVEN GREATER WORKS,** because I am going to be with the Father. You can ask for anything in my name, and I will do it, so that the Son can bring glory to the Father. **YES, ASK ME FOR ANYTHING IN MY NAME, AND I WILL DO IT!**
>
> — John 14:12-14

- **accepting there are things we can't explain.** That's what faith is all about. It doesn't mean you check your brain at the door or ignore the world's ever-growing bank of discoveries. It means coming to grips with our human nature, which isn't divine. We are not God.

That's why we trust the Holy Spirit.

It's dangerous and scary—and it goes against everything our culture teaches. But to trust the Holy Spirit means we can't cling tightly to our plans.

Our greatest successes at Group Publishing have come when we've trusted God.

When we developed the Sunday school Hands-On Bible Curriculum, we trusted God to show up through active learning. We tested lessons, watching noisy, active kids in classrooms that, by typical standards, looked out of control. But we used Jesus' teaching technique of using common, everyday objects to help cement biblical truths. To our amazement, kids were able to recall Bible points weeks later. We learned the difference between relying on our humanity and trusting the divine as emphasized in 1 Corinthians 1:25: "This foolish plan of God is wiser than the wisest of human plans, and God's weakness is stronger than the greatest of human strength."

A few years later, we set up a Bible-times marketplace called Holy Land Adventure, where children and adults have an opportunity to choose which project to work on. They can spend all their time in one shop or bounce from one to another. For those of us who love to be in control, the idea of giving kids so much choice seemed unmanageable and dangerous. But children and adults love it. It really works!

Holy Land Adventure provided lots of opportunities to let God work. In part of the marketplace, we planted shopkeepers who objected to the faith. They could say, "I believe in Zeus" or "Jesus is a fake." You might think it's outrageous for those words to be spoken in an environment in which learning biblical truth is the goal. But it was incredibly powerful in growing kids' faith. It provided a real opportunity for kids to explain their own faith to the "unbelieving shopkeepers."

One more example: One of the questions people frequently ask about Lifetree Café is "Do you assign people to tables to 'stack the deck' to be sure there's a 'learned Christian' at each table?" We assure them we don't do that. We trust the Holy Spirit. We've heard hundreds of stories of people who have ended up sitting with people who share amazing similarities and life experiences. Who knows how many opportunities might have been missed if we'd tried to control the programs through our limited human endeavors?

> The inspiration arrives in a rough, bumpy, and earthy language that reveals God's presence and action where we least expect it, catching us when we are up to our elbows in the soiled ordinariness of our culture and when spiritual thoughts are the furthest thing from our minds.[8]
> — Eugene H. Peterson, *Eat This Book*

- **trusting the Holy Spirit.** This story came to us from a faraway friend in ministry who used Group's Seaside Escape materials for a women's retreat:

  "My husband and I are missionaries in Suriname, South America. We have been here about 30 years now and have facilitated many activities, but this was our first ladies' retreat.

  "At one point during the retreat, I was supposed to play the recorded sound of waves while the ladies were 'still before the Lord.' Just as I was about to do this, the power went out. But we got something better than the recorded sounds of the waves. We are in the tropics, so we opened the windows and the big sliding door to our meeting room. There was a loud thunderstorm outside, with some wind and rain. We listened to those sounds instead of the recording. All the ladies looked like they were deep in prayer and inner stillness. When the time was up, I couldn't bear to interrupt the ladies. As I waited a few more minutes, the storm abated. It seemed as if the Lord himself wanted to provide the 'sound effects' at exactly the right time, for exactly the right amount of time! That was very meaningful to us.

  "I just wanted to let you know this. I'm sure you have a lot of similar testimonies from others who used the retreat material. Of course, much prayer went into our preparation, and I'm sure from your side as you developed it."

Trusting the Holy Spirit means truly letting go of our own agendas and allowing God to do his work. That's really what DIVINE ANTICIPATION is all about.

- **being relevant—and realizing that God is relevant to everyone.** What is most relevant is most personal. Relevance is ultimately very personal—what applies to each unique individual and that person's relationships.

Unfortunately, the church has confused being relevant with being hip. Tamie Harkins, former chaplain for Episcopal Canterbury Fellowship at Northern Arizona University, describes it this way:

> A few words on relevancy: making your church hip and trendy (coffee bar; free wireless; pastor with tattoos and ripped jeans) will probably draw in the young people. If your only goal is getting young people in your door, these things will work. Free alcohol will work even better (I guess you could advertise the Eucharist that way…). I don't have a problem with coffee, wireless, tattoos or ripped jeans, or thimble-size-sips of alcohol. It's just that, what do these things have to do with being relevant?

> Relevancy is about practices and conversations that address people's pressing and real concerns. Relevancy is about offering practices that help people come to peace with the death of someone they love. Relevancy is conversation about global warming and extreme poverty. It embraces discussions about technology (how to use it in ways that don't perpetuate the loneliness?), about sexuality (is polyamory—often known as "ethical, non-monogamy"—legit? how do you have a sexual relationship with someone who's been abused?), about polarization (how do I love my neighbor if my neighbor is one of those gun-waving, homophobic, whiskey-swilling, anarchist, neo-hippie, ex-convict types?). Relevancy also means looking around the community and the world, noticing who's marginalized and oppressed—because that's where Jesus put his attention—and finding ways to stand with and for those people. This "finding ways" is where the sole meets the trail, and that's where we've got to think creatively together.[9]

Amen to that.

- **expecting God to show up.** Whether 2, 200, or 2,000 gather in Jesus' name, God is in our midst. That's a promise.

But we have a tendency to equate large numbers with success. (If we stop to remember that we have an all-powerful, almighty God who showed up as a baby in a manger, why should we be frustrated if we don't draw large crowds?) Small numbers might disappoint us, but God might be revealed most potently at those times. After all, when we draw a big crowd, those are the times that tempt us to think, "Hey, look what *we* did!" Sometimes it's when only a few people show up that God really reminds us of his power.

If we adopt DIVINE ANTICIPATION as one of our key strategies for loving others, then we absolutely must expect God to show up, even if—or, especially when—the crowds are as small as they can get.

If we expect God to show up, he will. Consider this story about an impromptu reaction to one of our Workcamp programs:

"The night's theme was 'Remain in me.' The room was dark. The only word left on the screen was *Remain*. People stayed put. After about 15 minutes, a group of kids went to the foot of the cross. After 30 minutes, more than 100 kids were on the floor surrounding the cross. Someone stood and prayed aloud; then others stood to pray. They said the Lord's Prayer together; then they all sang 'Amazing Grace.' After an hour and 20 minutes, they're still soaking it in."

If that's not God showing up—DIVINE ANTICIPATION—we don't know what is.

Tugboats—Innovators

Nine months ago we moved to predominately discussion-based preaching in our church, and it has been interesting to watch people learn to contribute through discussion when they have been so used to just listening. There have been lots of teething pains, but now it just makes sense.

Worship groups no longer stand on stage. Enough of singing praises to the worship team; we have incorporated them into the circle of people. Now the music comes from *within* the congregation, not *at* the congregation… it's a freaky journey, especially for the singers and musicians.

There are innovators out there, and many of us are like little tugboats: We look like we're irrelevant; we aren't looking for the lights or Christian fame. We are tugboats made for one purpose: to move huge ships that cannot and should not move by themselves. The type of ships that end wars, save nations. The church will move into God's purposes, but the huge ships, whether they're actual churches or just Christian mindsets, won't move by themselves because they can't. They need the tugboats to move them into position.

Our consumer experience of church has put us into a coma, one which we need help waking up from. What we do or don't do when we gather corporately is crucial for such a time as this.[11]   — L.L.

Jesus said, **FOR WHERE TWO OR THREE GATHER TOGETHER AS MY FOLLOWERS, I AM THERE AMONG THEM.**
— Matthew 18:20

- **trusting that God will do what only God can do.** We are in a miraculous partnership with God, who allows us to plant, water, and cultivate "seeds." But God is the one who makes things grow. I (Joani) grew up on a farm and know the difference between the farmer's job and God's job. As hard as they work at planting and harvesting crops, farmers can't make a plant grow. It's a miracle. In the church we try so hard. We want things to happen according to our schedule. But we need to step back more often and watch God make our efforts grow.

> "After all, who is Apollos? Who is Paul? **WE ARE ONLY GOD'S SERVANTS THROUGH WHOM YOU BELIEVED THE GOOD NEWS.** Each of us did the work the Lord gave us. I planted the seed in your hearts, and Apollos watered it, but it was God who made it grow. **IT'S NOT IMPORTANT WHO DOES THE PLANTING, OR WHO DOES THE WATERING. WHAT'S IMPORTANT IS THAT GOD MAKES THE SEED GROW.**"

— 1 Corinthians 3:5-7

185

- **telling others—in an authentic, natural way—what God is doing in our own lives and in the lives of others.** When Christians start sharing what God is doing every day in our lives, we invite others to participate in our DIVINE ANTICIPATION. Not in a preachy sort of way, but in a natural "Oh, by the way…" sort of way.

  But the church has turned evangelism into a scary prospect—a sales pitch or a dire warning or an invitation to a secret club. We offer evangelism courses and sermons on what to say and how to say it. Regular people are afraid they'll say the wrong thing. After all, they're not the ministry "professionals."

  There's a much better way. God has equipped us with his Holy Spirit simply to tell our own stories—the good, the bad, and the real. The best part is that no one can argue with our stories of how God has intersected our lives. And when others realize they don't need a degree in evangelism, they feel empowered to tell their own God-stories. It's not complicated. Maybe the early church thrived because they didn't pay people to be professional "church people"—they were it.

- **allowing people to express their faith in their own ways.** Sometimes the church's rituals turn into outward *expected* shows of people's faith. We raise our hands, kneel, cross ourselves, clap, don't clap, stand, sit, close our eyes, nod, and sing along. We've designed a batch of physical actions that we assume equate with people's "buy in." These actions aren't bad or wrong (like the list of red flag words); they're just not dependable markers of DIVINE ANTICIPATION.

  How often do we interpret people's inner thoughts from their outer expressions? A number of years ago, we created a wall-building experience using newspapers and masking tape to separate small groups from each other. It demonstrated in a fun and memorable way how sin separates us. One woman looked very annoyed and wouldn't participate. We didn't pressure her to join in, but frankly our interpretation of her behavior was that she just didn't—or wouldn't—get it. Two days later she told us, "I was the one with the biggest wall." She was actually processing the experience in her own way as we, to our shame, were judging her. It was a powerful lesson for us about our own tendency to judge people's hearts by their behavior.

186

- **ritual and liturgy.** We may think of liturgy as only the rote rituals that Catholics, Episcopalians, Lutherans, and others perform. But many churches have simply replaced hymns and pipe organs with guitars, keyboards, and drums. In some ways, their worship leaders are as scripted as the liturgical prayers that have been repeated for a hundred years.

  Today's non-liturgical liturgies simply have a different face. They look like carefully timed sermons, countdown videos, planned music sets that conclude with the worship leader praying as the band plays softly in the background. You get the picture. There's no DIVINE ANTICIPATION in any of that.

- **a show.** Instead of stained glass windows and breathtaking cathedrals, churches today have used their artistic and talented staffs to create highly produced shows that rival the best rock concerts. They're multimedia extravaganzas full of flashing lights, pounding music, and theatrical fog. Churches have turned their attention to professionally produced videos and sermons that conclude right on time so the next group of people can exchange seats with the previous worshippers.

  People today might question the extravagance of churches in days gone by. How could poor people give their offerings to build and support ornate churches while they lived in squalor? No question about it, they may have missed out on growing a relationship with God. But could our churches today be doing the same thing in a different way? Maybe our large buildings, top-notch technical equipment, multi-sites, and polished worship services reflect the same kind of extravagance that prevents people from truly experiencing God on a personal level. Perhaps the spiritual squalor is no less prevalent.

- **numbers.** Remember, where two or three are gathered in Jesus' name, he'll be there, too.

- **signed confidentiality forms.** In some churches, the first thing small groups are asked to do is sign a confidentiality pact. These well-meaning Christians gather with other Christians to share their lives in a safe place. So they agree to keep secret whatever is shared in the group. (Not much different from "What happens in Vegas, stays in Vegas"!) The intention of confidentiality forms is to automate trust and halt gossip. However, the unintended consequence may have contributed to the church's decline by inadvertently preventing people from sharing what God is really doing in their lives and in the lives of their friends.

189

God's miraculous interventions, comfort, joy, peace, and hope are told though real people's stories. Not clever illustrations or jokes from the pulpit, but through regular people living life…and sharing it with whoever will listen.

So how can we incorporate DIVINE ANTICIPATION in our daily church lives? At first blush it might be hard to think of this act of love in practical terms. But we've got lots of realistic, doable suggestions in the next chapter.

Read on!

Endnotes

1. The Barna Group, "What People Experience in Churches," January 9, 2012, http://www.barna. org/congregations-articles/556-what-people-experience-in-churches.html.

2. Lifetree Café, "Lifetree Café National Attendance Report," compilation of ongoing annual survey results, snapshot taken May 2013.

3. Francis Chan, *Forgotten God* (Colorado Springs, CO: David C. Cook, 2009), 15.

4. Ibid., 142.

5. Ibid., 16-17.

6. Eugene H. Peterson, *Eat This Book* (Grand Rapids, MI; Eerdmans Publishing, 2006), 160.

7. Jim Cymbala, *Fresh Wind, Fresh Fire* (Grand Rapids, MI: Zondervan, 1997), 140.

8. Eugene H. Peterson, *Eat This Book* (Grand Rapids, MI; Eerdmans Publishing, 2006), 160.

9. Tamie Harkins, "Making the Church More Accessible to Folks Under 35," *Calling* (blog), April 19, 2011, http://www.fteleaders.org/blog/entry/practical-ideas-making-the-church-more-accessible-to-folks-under-35.

10. Eugene H. Peterson, *Eat This Book* (Grand Rapids, MI; Eerdmans Publishing, 2006), 67.

11. Adapted from Liz Lapsley, September 20, 2012 (9:14 p.m.), comment on Thom Schultz, "What Church Looks Like—in 10 Years," *Holy Soup* (blog), July 25, 2012, http://holysoup. com/2012/07/25/what-church-looks-like-in-10-years.

12 PRACTICAL WAYS TO LOVE WITH DIVINE ANTICIPATION

Loving others through DIVINE ANTICIPATION ISN'T MYSTERIOUS.

It's something we can all do all the time with anyone. Here are some hands-on things you can do to put DIVINE ANTICIPATION to work in your church ministry.

EMBRACE YOUR WEAKNESS So God Can Be Glorified

Don't view your weaknesses as shortcomings. View them as reasons to trust God even more. That surely leads to a complete trust in prayer and God's power. And that's DIVINE ANTICIPATION.

We appreciate what our friend Dave Cook said in launching his Lifetree Café: "God will bless weakness, but he won't bless carelessness. If you do what you can, God will do the rest. This was certainly true in our case because we weren't perfect, but God certainly did help us in our launch."

> "For the foolishness of God is **WISER THAN HUMAN WISDOM**, and the weakness of God is **STRONGER THAN HUMAN STRENGTH**."
>
> — 1 Corinthians 1:25

> "I also believe that the Spirit is more obviously active in places where people are desperate for Him, humbled before Him, and not distracted by their pursuit of wealth or comforts (like we are).[1]
>
> — Francis Chan, *Forgotten God*

SOFTEN Your Heart

It's not easy to admit that we might not be as open to loving others—and open to God's action—as we might wish. Most folks (including us!) tend to overestimate just how soft their hearts toward others really are.

Examine how much you really love people by answering the following questions. Then do it again in a few months. Then again a few months later. See how God changes you and others to be more like Jesus.

We have asked ourselves these questions periodically for the last few years, and we've discovered that God is continually changing us. Thanks be to God!

Reflect on your love for people. Rate yourself.

Can you overlook un-Christ-like attitudes and lifestyles in your efforts to connect with others?

1   2   3   4   5   6   7   8   9   10

Are you able to suspend your judgment for long periods of time around not-yet Christians?

1   2   3   4   5   6   7   8   9   10

Do you consistently seek to understand the not-yet Christians you know before seeking to be understood by them?

1   2   3   4   5   6   7   8   9   10

Are you patient enough to wait for the not-yet Christians in your life to ask for your opinion?

1   2   3   4   5   6   7   8   9   10

Be honest: Do you *like* people who are far from God?

1   2   3   4   5   6   7   8   9   10

Do people who are far from God like *you*? For example, are you invited to "party-parties"?

1   2   3   4   5   6   7   8   9   10

Does your body language communicate an open-hearted acceptance of the not-yet Christians in your life?

1   2   3   4   5   6   7   8   9   10

Are you able to communicate acceptance to not-yet Christians without endorsing their lifestyles?

1   2   3   4   5   6   7   8   9   10

In your relationships with not-yet Christians, do you typically offer kindness rather than "rightness"?

1   2   3   4   5   6   7   8   9   10

Is your heart consistently broken and filled with compassion for the not-yet Christians in your life?

1   2   3   4   5   6   7   8   9   10

85 to 100—Congratulations! You might be frequently misunderstood by Christians, but the not-yet Christians in your life are undoubtedly drawn toward the heart of Jesus formed in you. Keep walking in this light.

65 to 85—You must decrease, and Jesus must increase—one heart attitude at a time. Embrace the people and the situations in your life as God attempts to prune those heart attitudes that are not bearing fruit for his kingdom.

Under 65—Jesus needs to do something *in* you before he can do something *through* you. Consider spending less time doing religious activities, and more time asking God to do the soul surgery needed to form the heart of Jesus in you.

Excerpted from *God Space* by Doug Pollock.[1]

PRACTICAL WAYS TO LOVE WITH **DIVINE ANTICIPATION**

Make a Beeline
TO THE CROSS

In his book *Jesus-Centered Youth Ministry*, Rick Lawrence explores what it means to make a beeline to the cross:

> "If you think you can walk in holiness without keeping up perpetual fellowship with Christ, you have made a great mistake. If you would be holy, you must live close to Jesus."
>
> — Charles Haddon Spurgeon

Spurgeon was a 19th-century English pastor who suffered from depression and a painful birth defect. He preached two services every Sunday in his London church, each with a crowd of 6,000 people attending (this was before the invention of microphones). At the time, he had more books in print than any other living person. He still has more books in print than any other pastor in history, including more than 2,500 of his published sermons. Historians call him the "Prince of Preachers," and his remarkable story holds the key to Jesus-centered [ministry].

Spurgeon was born in England and committed his life to Christ in 1850, when he was 15 years old. He preached his first sermon a year later and took on the pastorate of a small Baptist church a year after that, at 17. Just four years after his conversion, the 20-year-old Spurgeon became pastor of London's famed New Park Street Chapel. A few months into his new position, his skill and power as a preacher made him famous—at 22 he was the most popular preacher of the day.

Much later in Spurgeon's ministry, a young pastor asked him to listen to him preach and give him a critique—a common request since Spurgeon was revered by other preachers. After he listened to the young man's impassioned sermon, Spurgeon was honest—he thought the sermon was well prepared and well delivered, but it nevertheless…stunk.

"Will you tell me why you think it a poor sermon?" asked the young pastor.

"Because," said Spurgeon, "There was no Christ in it."

The young man said, "Well, Christ was not in the text; we are not to be preaching Christ always, we must preach what is in the text."

The old man responded, "Don't you know, young man, that from every town, and every village, and every little hamlet in England, wherever it may be, there is a road to London?"

"Yes," said the young man.

"Ah!" said the old preacher, "and so from *every text* in Scripture there is a road to the metropolis of the Scriptures, that is Christ. Dear brother, when you get to a text, say, 'Now, what is the road to Christ?' and then preach a sermon, running along the road towards the great metropolis—Christ."

Spurgeon called this "making a beeline to Christ." It was his central, guiding commitment every time he opened his mouth to speak or teach or write.

He wrote: "Jesus is The Truth. We believe in Him—not merely in His words. He is the Doctor and the Doctrine, the Revealer and the Revelation, the Illuminator and the Light of Men. He is exalted in every word of truth, because he is its sum and substance. He sits above the gospel, like a prince on his own throne. Doctrine is most precious when we see it distilling from his lips and embodied in his person. Sermons are valuable in proportion as they speak of him and point to him. A Christless gospel is no gospel at all and a Christless discourse is the cause of merriment to devils."

Spurgeon's passion for Jesus, and his determination to track everything he said and did back to "the metropolis of Christ," is really the central—but unexplored—imperative in [ministry] today. What would a [ministry] look like that proactively found a beeline to Jesus for (literally) everything it did?[3]

You can help others "connect the dots" and make a beeline to Jesus in their daily lives.

You can make a connection to Jesus in something as mundane as doing the dishes or as profound as giving birth to a baby. How might these daily occurrences connect with Jesus—and make a beeline to the cross? Washing dishes can be a picture of Jesus' forgiveness. A newborn can be a sign of new life in Christ.

Share GOD SIGHTINGS

One of the most fulfilling skills you can hone as a Christian is watching for and sharing what God is doing in your life and in the lives of those around you.

We instill the practice of sharing God Sightings every summer during VBS as children and adults tell about ways they've seen God in action. At the close of each day of service, our Workcampers tell of their God

Sightings. Each week we watch God orchestrate who sits with whom at Lifetree Café and marvel at God's hand in their conversations. Every evening participants in Lifetree Adventures (our international mission trips) tell about instances from the day in which they saw God's handiwork. Most of our curriculum lines include a weekly time for students to share their God Sightings. God Sightings are a tangible, powerful way for people to give God credit. They're also a compelling way for God to reveal himself to those who question if he even exists.

We fully believe in and nurture DIVINE ANTICIPATION in just about everything we do at Group. Like invisible radio waves, we know God is actively involved in our lives—we just have to tune in.

Here are a few examples:

- We've seen God Sightings point children to Jesus even when life is terribly hard. One of our ministry friends told us a story about a family whose youngest daughter, age 6, was struck by a car and killed:

  "We arrived before the ambulance. God has given them such strength. We stayed at the house with the kids while the parents went to the hospital in the ambulance. It was almost four hours before they got home. Their 10-year-old daughter, Abi, sat on my lap and cried and cried as we waited and prayed for Aimee.

  "When she stopped crying she said, 'Mrs. Wood, I hope I have the best God Sighting ever to share Sunday.' A few hours after she learned her sister had gone home to be with Jesus, I heard her say to a friend, 'Wait, I do have a God Sighting. Aimee is with Jesus; I wish I could be with him, too.'"

  That's the kind of comfort only God can provide, and even young Abi could see God's hand in their horrible situation.

- In the early days of testing Lifetree Café, I (Joani) sat at a table with a man who happened to be new in town, having just rolled in on his motorcycle. As the conversation unfolded, I learned his name was Doug and that he was a former teacher who had traveled the world and loved the concept of Lifetree Café. As God would have it, Doug is now an important member of our Lifetree team. He lives in Washington, D.C., at the epicenter of politics, power, and connections. He brings a totally different perspective, which has been invaluable to our team. He participates every week in shaping our Lifetree episodes and researching interviews and stories. Why did Doug sit at my table? Because divine orchestrations happen every week, and we've learned (and are still learning) to be in tune whenever God shows up. It can happen every week in your ministry, too, when you're open to what God is up to.

- One summer we were visiting a Workcamp in another part of the country. We could be there only for the evening program. It was dark, and we were walking in the rain on a sidewalk to the gym with the director of the camp. Someone behind us asked if I was Joani Schultz. We learned she was from Hudson, Wisconsin. "Do you remember Lori Madden?" she asked.

  I said, "Of course, she was a great kid in my youth group 24 years ago." I learned the woman was here with Lori, who'd brought a youth group to this Workcamp, including her own two teenagers. Lori and I reunited after the program, and she asked me about my dad, who was celebrating his 75th birthday that year. She remembered counting 50 things for my dad's 50th birthday gift. Amazingly, on the way to the camp, she had told her kids that story about my dad. It was a remarkable blessing to reconnect with Lori, and we immediately recognized that God had brought us together for that special moment.

- Our friend Nick received this email from a friend in ministry following our Sky themed VBS program in which one of the Bible points was "No matter what happens…trust God":

  "We had such a blast with Sky VBS this summer! One story that I'd like to share with you is something that happened post-VBS. An 8-year-old boy who attended VBS was on his way to the operating room to get his appendix taken out. He was scared, so his mom tried to comfort him by praying with him. Then the little boy said, 'It's going to be okay, Mom, because no matter what happens I'm going to trust God.' It still makes my eyes a little misty thinking about how awesome our God is and how he can use one week of VBS to have such an impact on a child's life."

Canaanite religion was all about gods and their adventures. If you wanted in on it you engaged in magical manipulations—impersonal, nonrelational, acquisitive religious technologies. While their Canaanite neighbors were elaborating their wonderful myths of sky gods, thunder gods, and fertility gods and goddesses off somewhere in the far north, Israel was telling stories of their ancestors whose names they knew and in whose land they lived, ancestors who listened to and understood God present and personal to them in their everyday lives. God was present and active among them. Local and ancestral history, not legendary mythic worlds, was where they learned to deal with God. Their stories were rooted in the family history of their parents and grandparents. By implication they were included.

Myths are a way to create an imaginative world in which we can visualize the gods, put them on stage and see them at work, and then, by employing magical rituals and incantations, try to get them to work for us. It is all out in the open; there is no mystery. Neither is there any personal relationship—the gods couldn't care less about us; our only recourse is to bribe or manipulate them in some way or other. You may know the names of the gods and goddesses, but they don't know yours. Stories, in contrast, are restrained, respecting the reclusiveness and silence of God, letting God work and be in God's own way, respecting the essential mystery of his being and testing his goodness and providence in our lives.[4]

— Eugene H. Peterson, *Eat This Book*

Provide Abundant Time for "REGULAR PEOPLE" TO TELL THEIR STORIES

If they're honest, many churchgoers will admit they've "heard it all before." One sermon may elicit stifled yawns more than anything else. But when a regular person is given time to share a personal faith story (some call this a testimony), people perk up. We "regular folks" long to hear about God's activity in the lives of people like us. We all hunger for the wonder, awe, and reassurance that God is actively involved in people's lives now.

Whenever people come together, spend the precious time they've given you to share stories of what God is up to. Remember, Jesus came to earth not only to fulfill Scripture but also to demonstrate that God is alive. The Word became flesh and dwelled among us.

Hearing others' stories is a way to experience faith as a living, breathing relationship. We can't have a relationship with an expired historical figure. We *can* have a relationship with the living God who shows up through people and the events in their lives.

198

Celebrate God Sightings
WHENEVER PEOPLE OF ANY AGE GATHER

Anyone—from preschoolers to grandparents—can share God Sightings.

Here's an example from a story shared by one of our friends in ministry after a Lifetree episode called "China's Dark Secrets" in which we explored China's one-child policy:

"My two little girls pray for the 'baby girls in China.' And to this day, every penny or loose change they find is immediately set aside for All Girls Allowed [a fundraising effort that encourages mothers in China to give birth to baby girls instead of aborting them].

"Monday, my 5-year-old, Elizabeth, lost her third tooth. The tooth fairy visited that night. When Elizabeth woke up and found $1 under her pillow, she jumped up and placed it with the rest of the money our girls have set aside for babies in China. Awesome!"

It's so exciting to see God at work in a recognizable way even among our youngest believers.

> Point out how learners can apply their learning immediately [...] within the training sessions to practice new learning. [...] Practice increases competence and confidence, both highly correlated with motivation to transfer learning to the job. [...] New learning can be applied.[5]
> — Harold D. Stolovitch and Erica J. Keeps, *Telling Ain't Training*

Trust God, Realizing **YOU DON'T KNOW WHAT GOD IS UP TO**

Release your grip on control, and watch as God orchestrates unexpected results.

We've seen this again and again with experiential learning. It's a true adventure, which means we can't predict the outcome. We have to be completely open to letting the Holy Spirit work. The Holy Spirit reaches each person individually in a unique and very personal way.

199

We've talked with enough friends in ministry over the years to know the church isn't a big fan of surprises. Some say all that "experiential stuff" may work for kids but adults are beyond that. Well, we can say with 100 percent confidence that experiential learning works just as well with adults as it does with children.

In one of our courses, we challenged pastors to use experiential learning in their sermons. One of our overachieving students decided to turn his church's sanctuary into the "belly of the fish." He darkened the room, blackened the windows, had fans blowing in a stinky fish odor. He came out dressed as Jonah. It was dramatic, multisensory, and biblical. Needless to say, his congregation never forgot the message that "if you run from God, you'll get in a stinky mess." But the story doesn't end there. Months later, a well-to-do businessman paid a visit to this pastor. He confessed that he'd just had the opportunity to make a lot of money on a shady business deal. All he had to do was sign some papers, and no one would know. With pen in hand, he realized that if he did this, he would get in a "big, stinky mess." He told the pastor, "That message changed my life."

Step back for a moment, and think about the risk that pastor took. He stepped out and tried something the church had never experienced before, and it turned out to be something unforgettable. In a sense, that kind of risk isn't really risky at all—it's simply trusting God to do what he does best.

Plan **SURPRISES**

Pastors, if you really want to give DIVINE ANTICIPATION a whirl, don't prepare a sermon one week. Instead, spend your preparation time in prayer. Devote the time normally dedicated to delivering a sermon to asking people to tell someone sitting beside them how they saw God last week (or not). Then ask if a few brave souls would come forward and share their stories with everyone. You might be astounded at what you discover.

The fact is, people need to be surprised. It's so easy to settle into our familiar, comfortable ruts and miss out on what God is doing all around us. Sally Morgenthaler paraphrases how Sharon Bowman explains this rut in Bowman's book *Preventing Death By Lecture*:

> The "brain secretary" puts the main brain on autopilot while doing a repetitive chore, such as driving a familiar route to work, Bowman says. It is an enemy of good teaching. "The brain secretary

is programmed to take care of the routine. It says, 'Been there, done that. I've got it covered. Your mind can take a hike,'" she says. If a dog darts in front of the car, the brain secretary "bangs on the door of the thinking brain," which clicks into gear. "You have to keep the learner's brain active," she says.[6]

Pray, Pray, **PRAY**

God wants us to be constantly connected to him, and one of the best ways to remain connected is through prayer.

Lead individuals and groups in prayer as a way to keep them tuned into DIVINE ANTICIPATION. It's entirely practical to pray before events, classes, and worship. Every week at Lifetree Cafés all over the country, teams stand behind chairs and pray for the people who will occupy those chairs. It sends a clear message to everyone involved that we fully expect God to show up and change lives. You, too, can challenge your teachers and leaders to pray in the spaces that your people will fill.

Remember, the 4 ACTS OF LOVE are all about loving others. DIVINE ANTICIPATION comes from knowing that God loves us and wants to make something special happen in our lives. Let's let him!

Endnotes

1. Francis Chan, *Forgotten God* (Colorado Springs, CO: David C. Cook, 2009), 17.

2. Doug Pollock, *God Space* (Loveland, CO: Group Publishing, 2009), 22.

3. Rick Lawrence, *Jesus-Centered Youth Ministry* (Loveland, CO: Group Publishing, 2007), 19.

4. Eugene H. Peterson, *Eat This Book* (Grand Rapids, MI: Eerdmans Publishing, 2006), 157.

5. Harold D. Stolovitch and Erica J. Keeps, *Telling Ain't Training* (Alexandria, VA: American Society for Training and Development, 2002), 53.

6. Sally Morgenthaler, "Presentation Addiction," *NRB Magazine*, February/March 2007, 66.

DIVINE ANTICIPATION is not...

- **what happens in one hour on Sunday morning.** What if we could expand our once-a-week Jesus to an all-the-time Jesus? Churches have boxed Jesus in and made God unattainable without the church's help. Think about it: Do most people know what a complete Christian life really looks, sounds, and acts like?

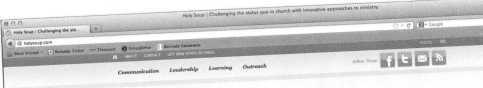

"It's About Sunday, Stupid."

A friend visited a large, famous church on a typical Sunday. The worship band performed with precision. The lighting and fog effects were state of the art. The pastor presented a polished sermon amidst specially built staging.

Later in the week, a pastor from this church shared their ministry secrets in a seminar. He described the staff's single-minded emphasis on excellence—for the Sunday worship services. He shared their internal mantra: "It's about Sunday, stupid."

We get the point. For many churches, the Sunday service is the initial introduction for the uninitiated. It's the main conduit for new members. It's the only time most churches ever see the majority of their people. It's the culmination of a week (or more) of staff planning and rehearsing.

We get it. But we fear this laser focus on the Sunday service is slowly anesthetizing the church and clouding its real mission. It's no wonder that many people come to worship for an hour on Sunday and then fail to live their faith once they leave the church building.

We're afraid it's too easy for an It's-About-Sunday-Stupid (I-ASS for short) church staff to begin to shade its mission toward merely filling seats on Sunday morning. That's not the same as a clear mission to bring individuals closer to Jesus, to transform their lives, to provide relational support for the body of Christ.

Instead, the I-ASS mentality can send the unfortunate, subtle message that the ministry is really all about the show—and its showmen.

We pray the church is not about the show. We pray it's not about Sunday. It's about God—working in and through people—Sunday through Saturday. Everywhere.

We numb our people's sense of mission and ministry when we imply it's all about what the staff performs on Sunday morning. The weekly worship service is not the main event. It may be a reflection and a celebration of the main event, which is God at work every day in and through his people. On the job. At home. At school. In the car. On the bus. At the store. On the field.

We need to expand our idea of church, of ministry. We need to shift more energy and emphasis into other, broader ways to be faithful to our calling as the church.

Church is not an hour on Sunday. Faith is not a staged show. Evangelism isn't the act of parking backsides in pews. Discipleship isn't the process of dispensing oratory to passive spectators.

We don't "go to church." We are called to *be* the church. Every day. Everywhere.

HolySoup.com

- **mass-produced "relevance."** You can't mass-produce relevance. As we said earlier, the church has a misguided understanding of relevance. It's not the latest technology, HD videos, contemporary songs, fair trade coffee, cool clothes, fog machines, or trendy designs and photos in bulletins and announcements. What is most relevant is what's most relevant to "me." It's not about an iPod, iPad, movie, Twitter, app, light show, or sermon reference to popular culture. The ultimate relevance is "me" and "my story." God wants to be linked to "me" in an intimate, loving way.

We design each Lifetree episode to be relevant to every person there. This report from one of our Lifetree friends describes one such evening:

"I was amazed as I watched God use two very different but equally broken people at my table to minister to each other. One told us that his girlfriend had miscarried that day and that he was having a hard time understanding and accepting it. Yet he told us how grateful he is for our church and how he's always felt accepted here, tattoos and all. Then I watched him minister to and comfort a woman at the table who was old enough to be his mom, as she sobbed because the filmed interview mirrored an experience she'd had with her daughter. It was truly God Space in action, and it was beautiful."

When your church ministry focuses on "me" and "my story," it sets the stage for DIVINE ANTICIPATION. God will show up in the most relevant ways imaginable.

- **an issue of biblical illiteracy.** Our culture's root problem is not a lack of biblical knowledge. The real problem is that people don't have a relationship with God in the first place. We need to realize that God is real and we can rely on him daily. In worship, focus on the reality of God and be awed by his presence.

- **rules.** Sometimes we think we have to say the right words and assume the correct body position as we pray and worship before God will show up. Bow your heads and close your eyes. Sit still, face forward, be quiet, look attentive. Sing with all the sincerity you can muster.

We also establish lots of religious rules in the hope of enticing God to show up: Take Communion with a pure heart. Attend membership classes. Bring your money. Etc., etc., etc.

God doesn't refer to a checklist we must follow before he joins us. When we gather as his church, God is always in our midst. God works miraculously through his imperfect people all the time.

188

The following pages detail 10 ideas for helping you incorporate the 4 ACTS OF LOVE into your ministry. All these ideas focus on the foundational theme that faith is a relationship. They're specific things you can do to live out RADICAL HOSPITALITY, FEARLESS CONVERSATION, GENUINE HUMILITY, and DIVINE ANTICIPATION.

1. Be a
"REGULAR PERSON"

Even God was willing to become a regular person. God came to us in human form as Jesus. Jesus was God showing us how to be human. Now we, as humans, can show others how to be like Jesus. We are the body of Christ—Jesus "with skin on." What made Jesus/God so astounding while he walked this earth? He interacted with humanity.

Like Jesus, ministry leaders need to interact with people in the mud and muck of their lives. It's way easier to hide out in theological minutiae and sermon prep than get messed up in people's lives.

So many leaders, especially pastors, don't like getting dirty. But it's time to become a regular person. Get real.

This is what it looks like: In a repainted storefront in Fort Dodge, Iowa, sits a Lifetree Café. Across the street is a budget motel that sells rooms by the hour. A block away is a women's prison. Homelessness abounds. Fort Dodge has seen more than its fair share of the down-and-out.

But it's also seen a mighty band of Jesus followers who are totally unafraid of getting dirty. They call their church Cana. Each Tuesday, noon and night, the doors open to welcome people who are black, white, Hispanic, homeless, college students, in rehab, alcoholics, disabled, on the staffs of other churches, and people driving BMWs.

And by unleashing the passions of these people, they've launched three nonprofits: an art studio, a halfway home for women emerging from rehab, and a horse-based psychotherapy ministry called Stable Connections.

By being a regular person and connecting with regular people, you can be well on your way to showering the 4 ACTS OF LOVE on people who haven't wanted to come to your church.

> "If it seems we are crazy, it is to bring glory to God. And if we are in our right minds, it is for your benefit. Either way, **CHRIST'S LOVE CONTROLS US...SO WE ARE CHRIST'S AMBASSADORS;** God is making his appeal through us."
>
> — 2 Corinthians 5:13-14, 20

2. Be a **MATCHMAKER**

What if we thought of our role as helping people fall in love with Jesus? Falling and staying in love with Jesus promises life, hope, passion, commitment, and joy—just like a great marriage. It's powerful. Merely doling out information about God isn't the source of that power. A real relationship with Jesus is.

As matchmakers, it's *not* our job to *make* people Christians. Our role is simply to connect people to Jesus. We set up the date. God's grace lights the fire. And the Holy Spirit takes it from there.

Too often we think the job is ours. Thankfully, it's not. Isn't that freeing?

An article by the Catholic News Service explains this idea of matchmaking further:

Harvard public policy professor Robert D. Putnam has a tongue-in-cheek suggestion for pastors: "Spend less time on sermons and more time arranging church suppers."

206

That's because research by Putnam and Chaeyoon Lim, assistant professor of sociology at the University of Wisconsin, shows that the more church friends a person has, the happier he or she is.

"Church friends are super-charged friends, but we have no idea why," Putnam [said]. "We have some hypotheses, but we don't know for sure."

The researchers found that nonchurch friends do not provide the same benefit in terms of well-being and that other measures of religiosity—belief in God or frequency of prayer, for example—do not serve as a reliable predictor of a person's satisfaction with life.

"People who frequently attend religious services are more satisfied with their lives not because they have more friends overall (when compared with individuals who do not attend services) but because they have more friends in their congregations," the two researchers wrote in the *American Sociological Review*.

And churchgoing alone without making friends does not improve well-being, they found.

"In short, sitting alone in the pew does not enhance one's life satisfaction," Putnam and Lim wrote. "Only when one forms social networks in a congregation does religious service attendance lead to a higher level of life satisfaction."[1]

What better way for ministry matchmakers to spend their time than simply setting up this kind of time for people who need Jesus? It's exciting to know that once we get friends together in Jesus' name, God will take it from there.

Throw Away the Key—
A Travel Parable From Russia

As our Russian tour guide walked us through the picturesque park, we noticed something strange along the water's edge. The railing along the walkway was covered with something odd. As we got closer, we saw that the metal bars were festooned with padlocks. Every imaginable design of padlock clung to the railings like flowers on a vine. What did this mean?

When couples marry in Russia, they take their wedding parties to the park. The beautiful couples pose there for photos. And then as a sign of the newlyweds' love and commitment to each other, they secure a padlock on the railing. Then they throw away the key in the water below as one more sign of their devotion.

What a great symbol of love and commitment!

For those of us who have committed our lives to being the bride of Christ, God calls us to throw away the key—to trust him completely. How can we, the church, show the world our commitment?

When it comes to putting love into action, will we say "I do"?

LET US BE GLAD AND REJOICE, AND LET US GIVE HONOR TO HIM. For the time has come for the wedding feast of the Lamb, and **HIS BRIDE HAS PREPARED HERSELF.**

— Revelation 19:7

3. Be a **RINGMASTER**

The ringmaster opens each show by shouting, "Ladies and gentlemen, boys and girls of all ages…" Something is about to unfold that will appeal to every person in the room. After the grand welcome, the ringmaster steps out of the way and lets the others shine. The circus experience is all about the team.

Jesus exemplified teamwork with his disciples. He wasn't a lone ranger, and you don't need to be one either. The people in ministry who make things happen are the ones who genuinely love others and what they can contribute. That means you might have to give away things you know you could do better. Like the ringmaster, you have to let go. Why is it so hard for us to let go when God himself has let go of so much by entrusting us with ministry? God is the ultimate ringmaster!

> "Ladies and gentlemen, boys and girls of all ages…"

In their great book *Renovation of the Church*, Kent Carlson and Mike Lueken write about the importance of imposing less of ourselves on our ministries: "Perhaps a hazard of Christian leadership is we don't learn how to listen. We spend inordinate amounts of time trying to inspire people to do what they may not want to do. We're always trying to persuade. We're constantly answering questions. We are doling out counsel. We pontificate. People would have benefited from having more of our ears and less of our mouths. There's a 'time to be silent and a time to speak' (Ecclesiastes 3:7)."[2]

No doubt, ministry *can* be a circus. But that's not exactly what we mean by being a ringmaster. A ringmaster leads the array of t[...]

invites "ladies and gentlemen, boys and girls of all ages" to join in the fun. The ringmaster isn't the show. The ringmaster makes sure the show goes on. The ringmaster delights in the spectacle, but the ringmaster isn't the spectacle.

In our experience, the most effective ministry leaders are equippers. That means they love others by equipping them to love. Irresistible churches have leaders who delight in helping and watching their team members love others.

4. Be a **SAFARI GUIDE**

We traveled to Namibia once and were eager to see some of the wild animals for which Africa is so famous. We climbed into a jeep driven by our weathered, bearded, dusty, experienced safari guide. We headed down a narrow road, which was actually a dusty riverbed. As we bounced along, our guide said he had a pretty good idea we'd see some wildlife along this route. He couldn't guarantee a sighting, but he thought our chances were good. And he was right. We saw lots of animals along the way.

Sometimes we saw the animals first. Sometimes, since our guide was so well trained, he saw the camouflaged creatures first and taught us how to spot them, too.

We trusted our safari guide. We knew he'd been down this path before. He may not have been able to promise us a sighting (we were in the open wilderness, not a zoo), but he ensured our chances were as good as they could be. He took as much joy in the journey as we did, even though he'd been on the journey many times before. He got a kick out of watching us make our discoveries.

Our job as leaders, teachers, and pastors is to guide people on a path of discovery. We lead them down the right roads, give them bits of advice here and there, and let them make their own remarkable discoveries.

5. **UNLEARN** Your ABCs

Many churches are measuring the wrong things. They've become obsessed with the ABCs: **A**ttendance numbers, big **B**uildings, and collecting **C**ash. It's all about numbers—not lives. All about easy-to-measure, visible "things"—not hearts.

We seriously doubt that any church leaders would ever consider themselves to be like the Pharisees, but the fact is, pharisaic thinking exists today and is all too common. The people Jesus lambasted were not the unbelievers as much as the churchy folks who claimed to have a corner on God, who obsessed with valuing outward, easy-to-measure stuff.

Don't believe us? Take a moment to dig into the Gospels and uncover what Jesus did in each of these instances. What did Jesus measure? What did the religious leaders measure? How would you compare Jesus' encounters with religious leaders to your encounters?

- Luke 11:37-40—The Pharisees were amazed to see that Jesus sat down to eat without first performing a hand-washing ritual.

- Luke 18:9-14—Jesus told the story of the Pharisee and despised tax collector.

- Matthew 21:33-46—When the religious leaders heard Jesus' parable of the evil tenants, they knew it was about them. They wanted to arrest Jesus but were intimidated by public opinion.

- Mark 7:5—The Pharisees and religious scholars goaded Jesus, asking why his disciples didn't "follow the rules."

- John 7:45-52—The Pharisees condemned people for believing in Jesus because they didn't know the law.

- Matthew 22:15-22—Jesus knew the Pharisees were driven by evil motives and called them hypocrites.

- Matthew 22:34-38—An expert in religious law tried to trap Jesus with questions.

- John 11:45-48—The religious leaders called a meeting to prevent a loss of their power.

- Luke 6:1-5—Jesus' disciples picked grain on the Sabbath, breaking another rule.
- Mark 3:1-3—The Pharisees watched Jesus carefully, trying to catch him breaking the law.
- Matthew 23:4-7—Jesus pointed out the Pharisees' love of power and prestige.

Everything Jesus did rocked religious people's world. Jesus made them uncomfortable. The Pharisees didn't like it because he laid bare their real values and put loving God and loving people above their sacred rules. They opposed Jesus because he dismantled everything they used to measure their own success.

Carlson and Lueken point out the futility of basing our ministries on numbers: "The difficulty is that we live in a church culture where external success is self-justifying. If more people are coming to our church, this is obviously a sign of success, and God must be pleased. The throng of people coming into the church is decisive evidence that the kingdom of God is advancing, or so we believe."[3]

At a time when churches' definition of success is based mostly on the "ABCs," it shouldn't be surprising that church leaders, in practice if not in word, treat churchgoers as consumers.

"This is the hard, raw reality of life in the North American church," Carlson and Lueken write. They continue:

The people who come to our churches have been formed into spiritual consumers. This is who we are. It is our most instinctive response to life. And you can hardly blame us. Almost everything in our culture shapes us in this direction. But we must become deeply convinced that this is contrary to the teachings of Jesus Christ, the one who invited us to deny ourselves and lose our lives in order to find them. If we do nothing to confront this in our churches, we are merely putting a religious veneer over consumerism and nothing is changed. We offer no real, viable, attractive, alternative way of living. And what is worse, our churches become part of the problem. By harnessing the power of consumerism to grow our churches, we are more firmly forming our people into consumers. *Pastors end up being as helpful as bartenders at an Alcoholics Anonymous convention.* We do not offer what people really need.[4]

Attendance. Buildings. Cash. Have these become your holy trinity? If you're not sure, just ask yourself these questions: When our church makes

212

important decisions, do our attendance numbers, our building, and our money play a major role in how we determine our future? When our church takes a look at its goals and successes, do the "ABCs" tend to take priority? If you answer even a reluctant yes to either of these questions, then you're probably measuring the wrong stuff. You're not alone—most American churches measure what's easy. It takes time and discernment and an entirely different kind of assessment to measure real life change and spiritual growth.

Attendance. Buildings. Cash.
Have these become your holy trinity?

We've learned that success is measured in stories, not statistics. And we hear real-life stories about spiritual growth week in and week out. These stories keep us focused on what God is doing through us. Seeing God truly at work is what we're all about.

Our friend Mikal Keefer understands exactly what that means. He sent us this note about an intimate ministry encounter:

"I was thinking about that whole 'nickels and noses' thing—what we tend to value as church board members. When you look at Jesus' ministry, very little of substance 'stuck' when there were crowds involved. Yes, Jesus fed thousands of people in a miraculous way, but these are the same people who a year or so later let him be crucified. Yes, the crowds gathered to cheer his entrance into Jerusalem, but where were those people a couple of days later when he was walking through the streets dragging a cross? Last night at Lifetree, I watched Cherie lean into a conversation with Brandy for more than 45 minutes, listening, talking, nodding, sharing. It ended with Cherie sharing her faith story, and when Brandy left, she called back to Cherie from the doorway, 'I don't think it was a coincidence I ended up at your table.'"

The value of Cherie and Brandy's exchange had nothing to do with attendance (crowds), church buildings, or how much money they were giving. It was all about loving others through Jesus. Period. Seeing those kinds of encounters every week is what drives us in our ministry. That's how we know God is working. In our book, that's success.

Measuring success by numbers can be very misleading. Just because your church is twice as big as the one down the street doesn't mean you're twice as effective. In fact, it may be quite the opposite. According to

Christian A. Schwarz, author and founder of the Institute for Natural Church Development (NCD International):

> The growth rate of churches decreased with increasing size. This fact in and of itself came as no great surprise, because in large churches the percentages represent many more people. But when we converted the percentages into raw numbers, we were dumbfounded. Churches in the smallest size category (under 100 in attendance) had won an average of 32 new people over the past five years; churches with 100 to 200 in worship also won 32; churches between 200 and 300 averaged 39 new individuals; churches between 300 and 400 won 25. So a "small" church wins just as many people for Christ as a "large" one, and what's more, two churches with 200 in worship on Sunday will win twice as many new people as one church with 400 in attendance.[5]

Also consider this: The third most common factor for decreasing evangelistic effectiveness is church size. Literally, the *larger* the church, the *less* effective it is at reaching the lost. NCD International research indicates that the third strongest negative factor to church growth is how big a church is. Schwarz found "the average growth rate in smaller churches was 13 percent over five years, whereas in larger churches it was a mere 3 percent."[6]

Not only does size matter (in the opposite way we think it does), but financial numbers are even less encouraging. Recent research calculated how much money it would take to reach certain cities for Christ using the traditional "attractional" model. You may not like the results:

> Just to reach one city alone would be astronomical and cost more than all Christian nonprofit ministries receive in a single year combined. For instance, the study shows that to reach Atlanta would cost over $63 billion. To reach New York City alone would cost more than $418 billion. Where would we expect such money to come from? Giving USA, a nonprofit foundation that studies philanthropy in the United States, in its 2008 giving report found $103.32 billion went to houses of worship and denominational organizations in 2007. That entire amount could only reach the greater Washington D.C. area and would leave the rest of our country without any ministry at all.[7]

A fair question to ask: Is the church spending its way into insignificance?

Even in Jesus' time, crowds were hardly a reliable measure of Christ's success. A scan of the Gospels reveals that the crowds amassed when they anticipated a miracle or two. But when they were challenged with the true call to follow Jesus, the crowds—and even many of his disciples—"turned away and deserted him." With a meager 12 disciples left, Jesus had to ask, "Are you also going to leave?" Simon Peter replied, "Lord, to whom would we go? You have the words that give eternal life" (John 6:66-68).

Following Jesus is not for the faint of heart.

> God is not interested in numbers. He cares most about the faithfulness, not the size, of His bride. He cares about whether people are lovers of Him. And while I might be able to get people in the doors of a church or auditorium if I tell enough jokes or use enough visuals, the fact remains that I cannot convince people to be obsessed with Jesus. Perhaps I can talk people into praying a prayer, but I cannot talk anyone into falling in love with Christ. I cannot make someone understand and accept the gift of grace. Only the Holy Spirit can do that. So by every measure that actually counts, I *need* the Holy Spirit. Desperately.[8]
>
> — Francis Chan, *Forgotten God*

> I also do not want people in huge churches to think that just because they have more people and more money that they are more blessed by God. The stats tell us that ten smaller churches of 100 people will accomplish much more than one church of 1,000.[9]
>
> — Neil Cole

So then how do we unlearn our ABCs? Here are a few ideas to get you on the right path to placing attendance, buildings, and cash low on the priority list:

- Quit measuring yourself and your success by the numbers.
- Stop asking numbers questions, such as…

  "How many people come to your worship services or classes?"

  "Are you doing multi-site?"

  "How big is your youth group?"

  "How many staff do you have?"

  "What's your budget?"

  "How large is your campus?"

- Review your church newsletters and bulletins. How much space is devoted to financial reports and graphs or rules about building usage?

215

- Audit your sermons and pleas for money. How often do you find yourself begging for dollars? Or worrying about repairing the roof? How often have you talked about a life that has been changed as a result of one of your sermons?

- Check how much time and energy are spent in committee meetings haggling over new building campaigns, fundraising, paint colors, carpet choices, and paving the parking lot compared to telling stories of lives touched through your ministry.

Just imagine what your church would be like if it left the ABCs behind and made the 4 ACTS OF LOVE the top priority.

> The outward success of our church came with a steep price tag. We had grown the church, but we were not more like Jesus. Growing the church did not require that we be like Jesus.[10]
> — Kent Carlson and Mike Lueken, *Renovation of the Church*

6. Forget **YOUR D'S AND E'S, TOO**

It's time to nix the words *discipleship* and *evangelism*.

The current meanings of these words have deteriorated from their original intent.

Let's start with evangelism. For most churches, evangelism boils down to one of two activities:

- Lecture a roomful of people about sin and God.

- Hope that stalwarts from your denomination move to town and join your church.

We've been contemplating the effectiveness—or lack thereof—of these approaches. Then we traveled to the cornfields of Iowa. There, a fledgling ministry called Cana exercises evangelism in a refreshing—and effective—way.

Real Evangelism

Barbara Huisman and a few of her friends talked about planting a church in their hometown of Fort Dodge, Iowa. They worked with their denomination to gain support, but they stipulated that they didn't want to follow the typical church-planting model.

Instead they dreamed of a "creative space where life and faith come together." So they leased an old downtown storefront location across the street from a budget motel that rents rooms by the hour.

While most church plants establish themselves with a Sunday worship service, Cana started with a Tuesday night Lifetree Café for a weekly hour of conversation about life and faith. If people are interested in a regular church service, Barbara refers them to the many churches in the community.

At Cana, the team demonstrates RADICAL HOSPITALITY. It's a highly relational approach that community members experience the moment they step inside.

Jodie, a woman struggling with addictive behavior, wandered into Cana's Lifetree Café one dark Tuesday night and was immediately embraced and invited to sit with Joyce, a Cana regular who enveloped Jodie with the simple love of Christ. Jodie said that night changed her life. The nonjudgmental acceptance overwhelmed her. "God went through me like lightning," she said.

Jodie experienced evangelism—true evangelism. Through relationship. With God's people and the Holy Spirit.

And then Jodie experienced discipleship. But not in the usual way.

Real Discipleship

Usually the church approach to discipleship means sitting through informational classes and sermons. But that's not how Jodie was discipled at Cana. She spent time with followers of Christ who lived out Cana's motto: "Where your passion meets the community's need. Where miracles happen!"

Jodie's miracles began that first Tuesday night. Her addiction ended that night. Week after week, God transformed her. She found her new and real identity in Christ. Cana's mentors surrounded her with God's love and guidance.

Then Jodie stepped forward and told Barbara she wanted to start a ministry. She wanted to form a recovery house for women struggling with addictions. It seemed like a farfetched dream. But Barbara and the people of Cana encouraged Jodie. They suggested she seek funding from local churches. So Jodie met with leaders at a local church—and walked out with a $50,000 commitment for the recovery house. Cana formed a new 501(c)(3) nonprofit organization, and the Gateway to Discovery women's center is on its way.

But that's not all. Other Cana people wanted to pursue their ministry passion for the arts. So they leased the space next to the Lifetree location to accommodate PieceWorks, a new nonprofit arts ministry.

Still other people at Cana found they shared a love for horses. So they established Stable Connections, another Cana nonprofit that uses horses for mental health therapy.

In just one year, this little ministry outpost called Cana has launched three new nonprofit organizations, a prayer ministry, and a community Bible study, in addition to Lifetree Café.

It's a picture of discipleship. Everyday people growing in their relationships with God, becoming active disciples of Jesus, carrying his love into the community.

In Fort Dodge, Iowa, evangelism and discipleship aren't an academic exercise. They aren't mass-produced. Instead, they're personalized and stem from authentic relationships. They're much like what Jesus modeled 2,000 years ago.

Making Divisions Where Divisions Are Unnecessary

The church has unintentionally created a caste system of people who are in the know (really, really in) and those who aren't (really, really out). That's no way to start and nourish relationships.

We are *all* Jesus' hands and feet. It was brilliant of God to set it up that way. Jesus is at the center of our lives, and our allegiance is to him. Jesus doesn't have two classes of followers. There should be no difference between a disciple and an evangelist.

When we set up Lifetree Café, we wanted a place where churchy people and everyone else realize we *all* have things to learn, to discover, and to admit. We don't delineate between the "haves" and "have nots." We've discovered that when we do that, those who "really, really know" discover that they really, really don't. This revolutionary outreach experiment is not only changing those outside the church walls, it's changing those on the inside, too.

When we think our job is to "close the sale," it's a sign we're thinking of faith as a transaction instead of a relationship.

Maybe We Should Eliminate the Word *Seeker*, As Well

One of our friends, Sheila, got feedback from a church staffer who didn't see a place to check "seeker" on the Lifetree comment card (instead of "member" or "guest"). Sheila told the staffer, "I'm a seeker. Don't we think all people are seekers?"

Honestly, any terms or labels that create divisions between our alleged levels of faith need to be eliminated. Part of our welcoming statement at Lifetree is "We're all in this together." Isn't that the truth?

> What good is the Good News if no one wants to listen to it? [...] If we're always trying to get people to behave right or believe right, that kind of takes the focus off of incarnation. God became human and lived among us, and we beheld his glory. That is present. It is ongoing. Realizing that changes the way you approach Scripture and the way you approach life. It takes the emphasis off of *doing* the right thing and puts it on *being* somebody authentic before God.[11]
>
> — Eugene H. Peterson

7. Let Go of **YOUR EGO**

Very, very few—if any—church leaders will admit to having an ego issue. Let's be clear: Letting go of your ego doesn't mean admitting you're arrogant, selfish, or vain. It doesn't mean that all you care about is yourself. But it does involve letting go of what you consider most important and allowing God to do what he wants.

Unhealthy egos have a way of choking a ministry. They inevitably turn attention toward the minister and away from the message, away from the body of believers, and away from God.

219

But unhealthy egos don't always recognize they're unhealthy. So here's a handy guide to help you detect a toxic ego. You know your ego is out of control if…

- more people refer to your church by your name rather than your church's name.
- your church's website features a dramatic picture of you holding a microphone.
- you calculate how to inflate your image with self-deflating humor.
- you maintain a reserved spot in the parking lot.
- you direct your fans to a website named after you, such as billysmith.com.
- you tweet things like, "I was humbled to see I was voted Most Popular Pastor." (Humble people don't cite their humility as they brag.)
- you convince yourself that you can handle any downsides of an oversized ego.

And anything else that places you or anyone on your team on a pedestal and away from loving God and loving others has to be considered a potential ego problem.

Jesus let go of his ego. He was God and he took on the nature of a servant.

Our egos poke through in lots of places. Most of us remain unaware of how much our perceived self-importance takes precedence in church ministry. Here are a few "ego alerts" to be aware of. If you catch yourself starting a sentence with any of these phrases, you may have some ego issues to deal with.

"Unless I do it myself…"

It seems to have become a badge of honor: "We don't use any outside resources."

Some people in ministry have decided to go it alone. They now spend a sizable chunk of their time creating their own curricula, Bible studies, teacher guides, devotionals, messages, music, videos, and artwork.

We've heard a variety of reasons for this, such as…

- "Nobody knows my people as I do. They have unique needs. I need to create material that's uniquely suited to them."

- "My church expects me to create everything from scratch. If I don't, they'll wonder why they're paying me."
- "Our church creates everything internally and brands it with our church name."
- "I like being creative. This is my creative outlet."
- "We can't afford professional materials."
- "The Bible is all I need. Give me the Bible, the whole Bible, and nothing but the Bible."
- "All the stuff on the market is garbage. I'm forced to create my own."

Though we understand some of the rationale, we're concerned about the final outcomes and some of the side effects of being a lone ranger resourcer. And we're concerned not just because we lead a publishing company. Sure, we're interested in seeing our resources widely used. But we have a deeper concern and love for the effective work of the local church throughout God's kingdom.

We, too, are consumers of resources in our work and ministry. We appreciate the perspectives, expertise, and hard work that others build into their resources. We learned a long time ago that we can get a lot more done and accomplish our mission better when we rely on others to supply us with what they do best.

That's true in our work, and it's true in virtually every other line of work. Successful professionals everywhere look to outside professionals to provide the tools they need to accomplish their missions. You don't find many doctors concocting their own pharmaceuticals. You don't find many carpenters making their own lumber and nails. You don't find many airline pilots refining their own aviation fuel.

Yet some in the church feel compelled to attempt to do it all themselves. And it's distracting them from what they're really called to do. Their justifications for shunning outside help could use some reexamination:

"Nobody knows my people as I do." That may be true. But in a largely homogenous society with access to mass communications, your people share more similarities than differences with the rest of the population. In the larger landscape, today's national brands, mass media, and franchises effectively connect with people in every community nationwide. Similarly, a good ministry resource connects with people in your church as well as people in thousands of other churches.

"My church expects me to create everything from scratch." If that's true, it may be time to adjust your written job description so that it focuses on ministering to people.

221

"Our church creates everything internally and brands it with our church name." Shunning anything that is NIH (not invented here) is less about excellence than it is about pride. As powerful (and ugly) as pride is, nobody comes to your church because you do your own manufacturing. They don't care about your branding. They just want to experience God.

"This is my creative outlet." Hopefully your ministry isn't about you. Find ways to exercise your creativity that do not deny your people more effective resources. Remind yourself of your desperate yearning to escape when you endured another homespun song that Devin felt "led" to share with the captive congregation. Don't be Devin.

"We can't afford professional materials." So, instead, you spend countless hours building your own. What's your time worth? Help your church prioritize its stewardship to support those efforts that directly affect your people's spiritual growth.

"The Bible is all I need." If that's ultimately true, your people don't need you; just hand them a Bible and go home. However, it's better to follow Jesus' example. He used a variety of ideas, people, and things to bring scriptural truths to life.

"All the stuff on the market is garbage." We understand. We've all been disappointed by inferior work. The world of ministry resources, like most other endeavors, includes a wide range of quality. There's some poor work, but there's also good work. Don't let the lackluster stuff keep you from finding and using good resources that will help you accomplish your mission.

The best ministry resources are created by gifted servants, pretested with actual participants, retested, refined, polished, and produced by seasoned teams of dedicated professionals. They're specialized members of the body of Christ who do their part so that others can do their part on the front lines of ministry.

And that's the true essence of the biblical picture of the body of Christ. Each part does what it does best. "If the whole body were an eye, how would you hear? Or if your whole body were an ear, how would you smell anything? But our bodies have many parts, and God has put each part just where he wants it. How strange a body would be if it had only one part!" (1 Corinthians 12:17-19).

God doesn't call any one of us to do it all, to be proficient at everything. He simply calls us to be the part of the body he created us to be. And to let others be the parts of the body he created them to be. So that, together, the body can accomplish the mission.

222

> # If you want to boast, **BOAST ONLY ABOUT THE LORD.**
> — 2 Corinthians 10:17

> A few years ago, when many people considered our church 'successful,' I was invited to a small gathering of pastors of large churches. We were meeting to learn how to become more effective leaders. It was, admittedly, a heady few days for me. I got to mix it up with some of the bigger names and up-and-coming stars in the large-church subculture. As we began our meetings, there was an unmistakable sense that we had to establish the pecking order among us. It didn't take long to discern who had the largest church, which church was growing fastest, which pastor was better connected, who was more nationally recognized, and so forth.[12]
> — Kent Carlson and Mike Lueken, *Renovation of the Church*

EGO ALERT!

"Unless I'm better when I compare myself to others…"

Beware: There will always be someone who's better or worse at certain things than you are.

There's nothing to gain by trying to outdo the next guy. It's a fruitless exercise that only subjects you even more to the tyranny of your ego. And yet it's one of the most tempting traps for people in ministry.

It's important to remember that this only becomes a problem when your ministry is performance based. When you focus on faith as a relationship and the 4 ACTS OF LOVE, comparing yourself to others isn't an issue.

223

> It's easy to take potshots at successful pastors. They are easy targets who get shot at a lot. But the issue of personal ambition is only more obvious with them, not more real or more sinful. Those of us who look longingly and with envy at our successful colleagues are equally, if not more, guilty of ambition. [...] It is time to admit to each other that it [pride] runs rampant in the religious subculture of our day.[13]
>
> — Kent Carlson and Mike Lueken, *Renovation of the Church*

"Unless I preach it..."

Church ministry does not begin and end with preaching. Similarly, neither does education.

College students learn a lot more from teaching assistants using interactive methods than from seasoned professors who lecture. So says a University of British Columbia study by Nobel Prize–winning physicist Carl Wieman. The study suggests that *how* you teach has far more impact on learning than *who* does the teaching. "It's really [more about] what's going on in the students' minds rather than who is instructing them," Wieman explains.[14]

"It's not the professor, it's not even the technology, it's the approach," adds Lloyd Armstrong, former provost at the University of Southern California and professor of physics and education.[15]

Wieman says that the need for a more hands-on teaching approach isn't a reflection of a generation raised on video games but has more to do with the way the brain learns. As far as professorial brilliance, there is "nothing magical about a particular person," Wieman says. "Lectures have been equally ineffective for centuries."[16]

Research shows that with even the most captivating speakers, people only remember 10 percent of what was said—if that.[17] Nonetheless, professors keep lecturing...and pastors keep preaching.

| 159 | 160 | 161 | 162 | 163 | 164 | 165 | 166 | 167 | 168 | 169 |

It helps to remember that your time with people is extremely limited. To illustrate this, take a tape measure and stretch it out 168 inches. Each inch represents one hour, so 168 inches represent a week (24 hours x 7 days = 168 hours). If we're lucky, people give the church one hour a week. (And most people these days are opting out of church.) This is a startling visual reminder of how little time we have to reach people in a classroom,

224

church service, or youth group meeting. We say we want changed lives, but we stubbornly cling to methodologies like preaching and lecturing that don't work, so ultimately we don't do anything to help people grow in their relationships with Jesus.

Just because everyone's doing it doesn't mean it works. For decades, research has proven that lecture-style preaching is not effective. Yet we cling to it because "that's what everybody does." The pyramid of learning has been around for decades.

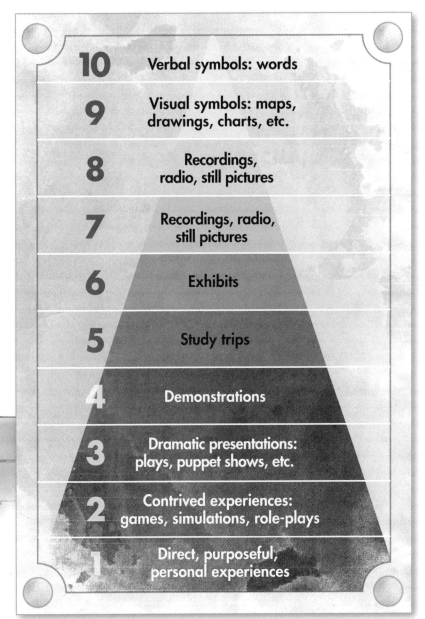

10 Verbal symbols: words

9 Visual symbols: maps, drawings, charts, etc.

8 Recordings, radio, still pictures

7 Recordings, radio, still pictures

6 Exhibits

5 Study trips

4 Demonstrations

3 Dramatic presentations: plays, puppet shows, etc.

2 Contrived experiences: games, simulations, role-plays

1 Direct, purposeful, personal experiences

"The Cone of Experience" from Audio-Visual Methods in Teaching, Third Edition by Edgar Dale, copyright © 1969 by Holt, Rinehart and Windston, Inc., reprinted by permission of the publisher.

When we realize that people remember up to 90 percent of what they *do*, we're compelled to make changes that will yield far greater results. We'll never lecture people into a loving relationship with Jesus. But we can join them, hand in hand, and experience Jesus together. That's what the 4 ACTS OF LOVE are really all about.

A victim of preaching?

" A young man named Eutychus was sitting in an open window. As Paul went on and on, **EUTYCHUS FELL SOUND ASLEEP AND TOPPLED OUT THE THIRD-STORY WINDOW.** "

— Acts 20:7-9

"Unless I create it myself..."

The church reinvents the wheel again and again and again every week. Right now some 300,000 preachers are preparing 300,000 different sermons for church services around the country. Stop and think about that for a moment. Does that make sense?

We can't help but ask three eye-opening questions:

1. Does the country possess 300,000 excellent writers who are capable of writing 52 outstanding scripts every year? (That's more than 15 million new literary pieces per year.)
2. Are the 300,000 congregations so different that each requires a customized sermon that's entirely different from every other congregation's?

3. If we started over today with a network of churches from coast to coast, would we deem it necessary to craft a different sermon for all 300,000 locations every week?

Imagine if the movie business operated in a similar fashion. What if every local movie theater felt the need to write and produce its own original film every week? Does every neighborhood possess excellent screenwriters capable of turning out 52 great scripts per year?

Sometimes people say, "But only our preacher knows how to preach to the unique needs of our congregation." Would that type of we-are-totally-unique thinking also hold true for your community's tastes in movies, books, television, and thousands of other products?

Every week 300,000 preachers each spend an average of 20 hours preparing original manuscripts (almost all of which are shared once and then filed away). What if we found a more efficient use for those 6 million hours of labor each week? What if most of those preachers used the scripts of gifted writers and redeployed their 6 million hours to direct face-to-face ministry and helping others actually grow closer to Jesus? Imagine how God might use those reclaimed hours.

Your act of creativity is not the goal.

8. Get
OUT OF CONTROL

We're not in control; God is. We don't save people; God does.

Crazy as it seems, God loves us and entrusts his world to us. God is a perfect parent. He's not a dictator parent or a helicopter parent. God sticks with us in the good times and bad, forgiving us again and again. He loves us and longs to be loved by us.

But too many leaders think if they don't do what they feel called to do, it won't be done right. Think how difficult it is for leaders to allow someone else to lead or speak. Entire church bodies hold so tightly to control, fearing they're the only ones interpreting Scripture correctly. God works through whomever he chooses. We must relinquish the idea that we're in control.

One of the questions people ask us most frequently about Lifetree Café is "Do people talk about what they're supposed to? What if they say something that's theologically incorrect? What if they say the wrong thing?"

We usually answer that question with another question: "What do people talk about when we leaders aren't around to correct them?" Any church leader who thinks he or she is actually "in control" is living in a fantasy.

Leaders create an environment for God's Spirit to work. That's what we control: the environment.

The Bible uses the metaphor of planting, watering, and growing to describe the process of drawing people closer to Jesus. God gives us the responsibility of planting and watering seeds, but God is the one who makes them grow (1 Corinthians 3:6). Whether we're talking about an oak tree or a person's faith, God is ultimately the one in control. Imagine planting an acorn and expecting it to sprout into a giant tree overnight. Most often the growth is slow, and that's what's hard for those of us who love the idea of being in control. Trust God. Trust the role he's given us. Trust.

9. FEAR NOT!

Fear is your worst enemy.

Our society seems driven by fear. We're afraid of everything, so we've surrounded ourselves with safety measures: seatbelts, helmets, knee pads, airport security, metal detectors, safe water, safe air, peanut-free zones, smoke detectors, carbon monoxide detectors, fire alarms, building codes, background checks, warning labels, TV channel blockers, movie and game rating systems, sex offender registries. We don't even allow our kids to play outside anymore for fear that a stranger will abduct them.

The church, too, is engulfed in fear:
* We fear naysayers.

* We fear the new and different.

* We fear change.

* We fear doctrinal impurity.

* We fear factual purity.

* We fear deeper relationships with people and instead pursue relationships with ideas.

* We fear not knowing all the answers.

* We fear losing our jobs. (Think about what's happened to churches that created a culture of control in which people feared their jobs, incomes, and livelihoods would disappear if they challenged the status quo.)

- We fear loss of control.

- We fear getting hurt. We don't want to be hurt again. (One pastor told us, "Relationships in the church inflict pain that's like a paper cut—it isn't life-threatening, but it hurts…it *really* hurts. So, to protect myself, I steer clear of relationships.")

- We fear that if we accept people whose choices aren't biblical, that means we endorse those choices.

- We fear failure.

No wonder the Bible says "fear not" 366 times—one for every day of a leap year!

Fear is stifling the church. It's keeping the church from fulfilling its potential.

And fear is often characterized by these nasty words: "That will never work." Those who utter these words have unknowingly been crippling the church—and many other endeavors. A few historic examples:

"Heavier-than-air flying machines are impossible." (Lord Kelvin, British mathematician and physicist, 1895)[18]

"The horse is here to stay, but the automobile is only a novelty—a fad." (The president of Michigan Savings Bank advising Henry Ford's lawyer, Horace Rackham, not to invest in the Ford Motor Company, 1903)[19]

"There is no reason anyone would want a computer in their home." (Ken Olsen, president of Digital Equipment Corporation, 1977)[20]

In other words, "That will never work." We've heard these familiar words in our church and from people in the thousands of churches we serve through Group Publishing and Lifetree Café. And we see these words echoed in comments to ministry bloggers who dare to suggest better ways of doing ministry.

At Group, we extensively test our ministry innovations to ensure they will indeed work. But that doesn't seem to faze the naysayers. For example, after we pioneered, tested, and proved that multi-age learning groups work beautifully in vacation Bible school, they still said, "That will never work." The tens of thousands who did try the new way, however, saw the immediate benefits, and they'll never go back to their old ways of doing things.

What makes it so tempting to slam the door on new ways of doing things? Here are typical comments:

- **"We've never done it that way before."** The seven words of a failing ministry.

- **"We tried that before. It didn't work."** It doesn't seem to matter if times or circumstances have changed.

- **"Maybe it worked for you, but it would never work here."** The often false assumption that the home team is hopelessly peculiar and out-of-step with the rest of humanity.

- **"I'm not comfortable with that."** A leader's unfamiliarity with a solution trumps the common good.

- **"It was good enough for my parents and grandparents; it's good enough for this generation."** A change, even if advantageous, might make the past or the status quo look deficient somehow.

- **"Who painted an 'S' on your chest?"** Pioneers of new ideas are snakes to be avoided, along with all their ideas.

These excuses, and many more, hold ministries back. The hasty, knee-jerk dismissal of anything new and different dooms a ministry to gradual decline. In fact, this kind of thinking is killing many churches.

Top Flops

At Group, we celebrate failure—as long as we learn from it. In one of our leaders meetings, we stood in a circle and each of us told about a mistake we'd made. To lighten the mood, we tossed a flip-flop sandal to the person speaking. That meant everyone—even we, the owners of the company—had to admit a mistake and tell what we learned from it. One new leader nervously admitted he'd been in a company where "heads would roll" if anyone ever 'fessed up to a mistake.

We believe mistakes are teachable moments. As long as we own up to our mistakes and don't repeat them, our top flops can be a good thing.

10. Just TRY IT!

Embrace a "let's just try it" attitude. A leader's willingness to say, "Let's just play with this and see how it goes" is incredibly empowering to a group. Too often we let history be our only teacher, and sometimes our own experiences can be our biggest obstacles.

When I was in youth ministry, my (Joani's) favorite line was "Tonight we're going to be guinea pigs. We're just going to try something." Creating an atmosphere in which everyone knows it's okay to fail frees participants to think, "Sure, I'll play along. It's all right if it doesn't turn out as planned." It frees everyone—the participants *and* the leader—to realize that whatever happens is okay.

If you, as the leader, are willing to take risks and give new things a try, people will join in. They really will! If you believe in it, they will do it. On the other hand, a skeptical vibe from the leader is a surefire way to doom the effort.

The importance of believing in new ideas has been a part of Group's culture since its very beginning. Group's story started with a 22-year-old kid, $500, and a typewriter. I (Thom) realize that if I'd known then what I know now, I would have thought it couldn't be done.

A Sunday school teacher using our FaithWeaver Sunday school curriculum was teaching a lesson that involved kids in making paper airplanes and tossing them at targets. As kids tossed the airplanes, they repeated, "No matter what happens, I can trust God." At the time, the teacher thought there was no place for such a frivolous activity in Sunday school. But she had a change of heart a couple of years later. One of the children from that previous class learned his mother had brain cancer. She died six weeks after learning the diagnosis. At the funeral, the little boy placed a paper airplane in the casket with his mother. He said, "No matter what happens, I can trust God." We're so glad the teacher took a risk and did something she assumed wouldn't work…because it did. No matter what happens, you *can* trust God!

It's been 40 years since Group started, and the same kinds of doubts are expressed about our newest endeavors, including Lifetree Café. We've heard lots of people say, "That's impossible." But nothing is impossible with God (Luke 1:37). So we just keep telling everyone who will listen, "Let's just try it."

Keeping the Guinea Pigs Busy

We test new ideas again and again, tweaking and adjusting them until we know they work. We test everything: Workcamp programs, VBS, curricula, Lifetree Café, and workshops. We're obsessed with getting feedback about how well our materials may or may not work.

For example, we field test each Lifetree Café episode at least four times with the public before we release it. We field test every full day of VBS materials a year in advance. We invite ministry leaders from across the country to experience the test and debrief each experience and every question.

One of the most popular elements of our vacation Bible school materials are our "field test findings": the ideas we thought would work, but didn't. We like to say, "We made the mistakes so you don't have to."

Honest feedback is ingrained in Group culture. That's why we can promise with confidence that our materials will work when they're used as written.

Frankly, we're stunned by ministry leaders who tell us, "I write my own" or "That won't work" or "I mix and match because I know my people." Churches insist on being their own lab scientists, which turns their people into unsuspecting guinea pigs.

Negativity Is a Curable Condition

We suggest a number of steps to cure this sickness.

1. Drop your automatic defenses. Take a breath. Resist the urge to immediately reject new and different ideas.
2. Own the fact that clinging to the same old methodologies will result in the same old results.
3. Listen to the pioneers. Consider the new and different with an open mind. Honestly investigate their references, record, research, and results.
4. Prepare your people. Invite them to join you in the adventure of trying something new. Tell them, "We're going to try something new. Let's see how it goes." If they know they're part of an experiment, they'll feel like partners, not victims.

5. Exude a positive attitude. If you demonstrate optimism, your people will pick up on your constructive desire to move forward. Positivity is contagious.

6. Expect results. Implement the new plan. Give it adequate time to succeed. Then honestly evaluate the outcome. Involve your people in the evaluation. Iron out the wrinkles. And celebrate a new day.

> "New wine **MUST BE STORED IN NEW WINESKINS.**"
>
> — Luke 5:38

Some Final Notes of
ENCOURAGEMENT

A Pew Sitter's Thankful List

The woman began to weep after we inducted her into Group's Sunday School Hall of Fame.

"I've taught for 50 years. This is the first time anyone stopped to thank me," she said.

Then we began to weep. Too often, paid and unpaid ministry leaders and workers serve faithfully with little affirmation or thanks.

Well, this is a good reason for us to stop and give thanks. We've received a lifetime of blessings from our church leaders and workers. We owe many thanks. Here are just a few.

Thank you for…

…knowing our names and the names of our family members.

…urging us to call you simply by your first name.

…spending time with our son, providing him with a formative adult Christian friend.

…demonstrating, through your life, how to keep the faith in tough personal times.

…praying for us.

233

…resisting the temptation to pass along gossip.

…your thoughtful handwritten notes.

…doing what's right, rather than what's denominationally correct.

…allowing volunteers to run with their ministry passions.

…your eagerness to learn—even from non-ministry voices.

…acknowledging your weaknesses.

…spending time on our turf.

…your passion for finding lost sheep.

…your active support of other staff members.

…sharing the stage with nonprofessionals who have their own God stories to share.

…remembering to say thank you—even when we forget to do the same.

Travel Parable From Antarctica

We often use incidents from our trip to Antarctica as teaching tools. (Maybe leaders listen happily to our stories and look at our photos because they're relieved they don't have to go there themselves!)

First we traveled to the tip of South America—the end of the earth—Ushuaia, Argentina. It's so far from civilization that, in the past, the Argentine government sent prisoners there to be as far from others as possible.

From the tip of South America, we boarded an expedition ship, and we noticed sick bags located every foot along the handrails. That was a clue! We traveled for two days across the most treacherous seas on the planet. We churned through menacing waves up to 50 feet high. Half the passengers stayed in their staterooms because they were sick.

The voyage took us to the continent of Antarctica (which doubles in size in the winter and partially melts away in the summer). Nothing grows on the rocks. Hardy penguins hoard their nests of pebbles, while sea lions, walruses, and other creatures live underwater. Icebergs are as magnificent as clouds. It's a deadly yet gloriously beautiful place. And it's here, in this unbelievably harsh environment, that scientists and researchers from countries all over the world work together and scientific breakthroughs occur.

The icebreaker ships nose their way through the ice to carve open a passageway, but their captains wisely know they can push only so far. Passengers know that things might not go as planned. They have to trust, live on faith, and accept uncertainty and change. But often it is glorious—and worth all of the discomfort of getting there.

How is this Antarctica adventure like taking your church to a place it's never been?

Some people don't want to go there. And some people are ready for the adventure.

God is with you!

A Prayer
FOR YOU FROM US

Love from the center of who you are; don't fake it.
Run for dear life from evil; hold on for dear life to good.
Be good friends who love deeply; practice playing second fiddle.
Don't burn out; keep yourselves fueled and aflame.
Be alert servants of the Master, cheerfully expectant.
Don't quit in hard times; pray all the harder.
Help needy Christians; be inventive in hospitality.

— Romans 12:9-13

Let Jesus' love make you irresistible.

HOW TO BECOME A **RADICAL, FEARLESS, GENUINE, DIVINE** LEADER

Endnotes

1. Nancy Frazier O'Brien, "Researcher's advice to pastors: Spend more time on church suppers," Catholic News Service, March 2, 2012, http://www.catholicnews.com/data/stories/cns/1200867.htm.

2. Kent Carlson and Mike Lueken, *Renovation of the Church* (Downers Grove, IL: InterVarsity Press, 2011), 166.

3. Ibid., 67.

4. Ibid., 68.

5. Christian A. Schwarz, quoted in Neil Cole, "Is Bigger Really Better? The Statistics Actually Say 'No'!" *Churchplanting.com*, http://www.churchplanting.com/is-bigger-really-better-the-statistics-actually-say-no.

6. Ibid.

7. Neil Cole, "Can We Afford to Leave the Work to the Mega Church?" *Cole-Slaw* (blog), August 11, 2012, http://cole-slaw.blogspot.com/2012/08/can-we-afford-to-leave-work-to-mega.html.

8. Francis Chan, *Forgotten God* (Colorado Springs, CO: David C. Cook, 2009), 143.

9. Neil Cole, "Is Bigger Really Better? The Statistics Actually Say 'No'!" *Churchplanting.com*, http://www.churchplanting.com/is-bigger-really-better-the-statistics-actually-say-no.

10. Kent Carlson and Mike Lueken, *Renovation of the Church* (Downers Grove, IL: InterVarsity Press, 2011), 40.

11. *The Gathering*, "Eugene Peterson: Master of the Message," Spring 2011, 1-2.

12. Kent Carlson and Mike Lueken, *Renovation of the Church* (Downers Grove, IL: InterVarsity Press, 2011), 75.

13. Ibid., 76-77.

14. Seth Borenstein, "Study: It's not teacher, but method that matters," *Washington Times*, May 12, 2011.

15. Ibid.

16. Ibid.

17. Jeff Slutsky and Michael Aun, *The Toastmasters International Guide to Successful Speaking* (Chicago, IL: Dearborn Financial Publishing, 1997), 53.

18. "William Thomson, 1st Baron Kelvin," *Wikipedia, The Free Encyclopedia*, http://en.wikipedia.org/w/index.php?title=William_Thomson,_1st_Baron_Kelvin&oldid=561095660.

19. "Horace Rackham," *Wikipedia, The Free Encyclopedia*, http://en.wikipedia.org/w/index.php?title=Horace_Rackham&oldid=541824496.

20. "Ken Olsen," *Wikipedia, The Free Encyclopedia*, http://en.wikipedia.org/w/index.php?title=Ken_Olsen&oldid=558241238.

after WORDS

THE TALK
OF THE
TOWN

How people experience God **REALLY MATTERS.**

Every day we hear stories from Lifetree Café, stories that reveal the miraculous ways God is moving in people's lives.

Wouldn't it be wonderful if churches collected life stories like this every day?

Here's a very small sample of some of the amazing stories we've received and witnessed in our ongoing experiment with Lifetree Café. We hope these true life accounts inspire you to see what a tremendous difference the 4 ACTS OF LOVE can make in your ministry.

> " "Taste and see that
> **THE LORD IS GOOD.** "
> — Psalm 34:8

"It's what I've been missing MY WHOLE LIFE."

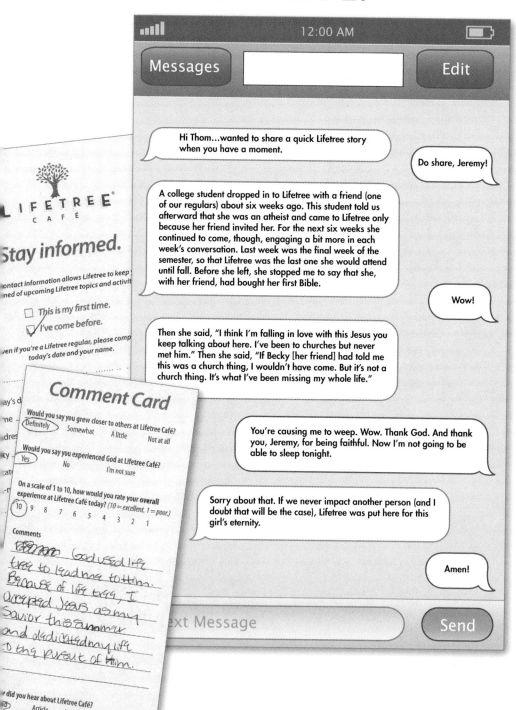

12:00 AM

Messages   Edit

Hi Thom…wanted to share a quick Lifetree story when you have a moment.

Do share, Jeremy!

A college student dropped in to Lifetree with a friend (one of our regulars) about six weeks ago. This student told us afterward that she was an atheist and came to Lifetree only because her friend invited her. For the next six weeks she continued to come, though, engaging a bit more in each week's conversation. Last week was the final week of the semester, so that Lifetree was the last one she would attend until fall. Before she left, she stopped me to say that she, with her friend, had bought her first Bible.

Wow!

Then she said, "I think I'm falling in love with this Jesus you keep talking about here. I've been to churches but never met him." Then she said, "If Becky [her friend] had told me this was a church thing, I wouldn't have come. But it's not a church thing. It's what I've been missing my whole life."

You're causing me to weep. Wow. Thank God. And thank you, Jeremy, for being faithful. Now I'm not going to be able to sleep tonight.

Sorry about that. If we never impact another person (and I doubt that will be the case), Lifetree was put here for this girl's eternity.

Amen!

Text Message   Send

LIFETREE CAFÉ

Stay informed.

...ontact information allows Lifetree to keep ...ned of upcoming Lifetree topics and activit...

☐ This is my first time.
☑ I've come before.

...en if you're a Lifetree regular, please comp... today's date and your name.

Comment Card

Would you say you grew closer to others at Lifetree Café?
(Definitely)   Somewhat   A little   Not at all

Would you say you experienced God at Lifetree Café?
(Yes)   No   I'm not sure

On a scale of 1 to 10, how would you rate your overall experience at Lifetree Café today? (10 = excellent, 1 = poor.)
(10) 9   8   7   6   5   4   3   2   1

Comments

God used lifetree to leading to Him. Because of lifetree, I accepted Jesus as my Savior this summer and dedicated my life to the pursuit of Him.

...w did you hear about Lifetree Café?
... Article   Newspaper Ad
...site   Mailer   Flyer   E-mail

A few months later we received this email from Craig, Lifetree's national director:

"Jeremy just called. He got home from Lifetree and said it was the most amazing evening ever. Remember Amber who was an atheist and wrote on her comment card just recently that Lifetree has changed her life and introduced her to Jesus? She now is a Lifetree fan and is inviting everyone at the college in town to Lifetree. Five new college students attended tonight, and they're all super excited about next week's topic! Yay, God!"

"Just loving everyone who WALKS THROUGH THE DOOR..."

God is doing amazing things at Lifetree Café! Let me share a bit of what he and the Spirit have been doing.

Now remember, we are a tiny church plant (with 75 to 90 people in worship each week).

In just the last six weeks, we've seen...

- 13 first-time visitors come to Lifetree for the episode about reincarnation.

- 9 new visitors from the community come to Lifetree for the episode about bullying.

- 1 gentleman, who has faithfully attended our Lifetree for a year, attend worship with us for the first time. (By the way, he's been a faithful part of other serving projects at our community center location.)

- the babysitter for our Lifetree Café, a local teen, attend worship for the first time with us. She brought 5 guests with her.

What's so exciting to us is not only that the Lord is bringing such a variety of individuals to our Lifetree Café, but also that conversations are happening and friendships are being made and our simple little group of believers (many of whom are themselves new to Jesus) are, with the Holy Spirit's help, just loving everyone who walks through the door. It's an utter delight!

I can't wait to hear how God will use Lifetree Café to grow his kingdom!

239

"God is using Lifetree to help **HEAL THIS FAMILY**."

Friends of mine recently lost their daughter to suicide. My wife and I had the blessing of sharing the message at the funeral. A week after the funeral, the father and son contacted us because they wanted to accept Christ. The mother hadn't been out of their house since the loss. Their family story is difficult (as many of our stories are), but God is bringing life out of death.

You could have knocked me over with a feather when the family walked into our Lifetree Café last night.

God is using Lifetree to help heal this family. God is doing a new work to prevent this from ever happening again within this family. If we couldn't do one more Lifetree Café, it would be okay with me. God just did it all last night.

"There are so many people there who **MAKE A DIFFERENCE IN MY LIFE**."

On the way to Starbucks, I ran into Kent in the parking lot. He asked me what I thought about today's Lifetree Café topic ("The Bible: Real? Relevant? Reliable?"). I explained that I didn't attend the noontime session but am going tonight. I asked him what he thought of the topic, because I was sure he'd have a lot of comments on the Bible's validity.

He said, "It was a good topic. But really I just love going to Lifetree, no matter what the topic is. I live alone and get lonely. There are so many people at Lifetree who I enjoy being around and who make a difference in my life. I just love going there."

I told him that we love him and we're glad he comes.

"She felt **WANTED AND IMPORTANT**."

Lori attended a Lifetree episode called "To Heaven and Back," the story of young Colton Burpo's trip to heaven where he sat on a small chair next to Jesus. During the "befriending" time, people were asked to choose their favorite chair: a beach chair, a recliner, or a kitchen chair. Lori said her favorite chair was the chair she was sitting in at Lifetree. She said she felt wanted and important at Lifetree. She also said she never has a chance to be a "queen" at home but feels like one at Lifetree. All that to say…little Colton's encounter with the throne of God is not that far off.

"**ONLY GOD** can do this kind of work."

For me, the most amazing thing about Lifetree is watching God move so visibly in that room week after week. God puts just the right people at just the right tables. Here are some examples…

A dad and son attended Lifetree for the first time. The son had just gotten his second DUI. They "happened" to sit with one of our Friendship Team members, whose son had experienced the same thing.

In another episode, we were asked to talk about God's ability to bring something that was dead back to life. A gentleman at my table responded, "That's exactly where my wife and I are right now."

A woman who has started attending regularly said at the end of one episode, "I want to know Jesus like that." That very night, she prayed to receive Jesus in her heart. Only God can do that kind of work.

In 20 years I've never been part of a ministry in which I've trusted God more. I've watched his followers be used to create real God Space, where he moves in miraculous ways week after week.

"We've touched **OVER 1,000 LIVES**…that we would have never encountered otherwise."

In the winter of 2008, our church started on a journey. We wanted to discover where God was leading our church and how he might want us to change. During the next couple of years, a core group met monthly to discover a new vision for our church. As we were searching, God revealed to us that we had lost our first love. We had become a church whose focus was more on ourselves than on God and others. We loved Jesus but had drifted away from sharing him with people outside the church.

In the spring of 2010, our youth pastor told us about a new ministry called Lifetree Café. It sounded like exactly what God was calling us to do. God had provided a way for us to move out into our community with a ministry that would reach those who might never come to a church. At the same time, Lifetree Café would help us become more comfortable talking about faith issues with our neighbors.

It wasn't easy. Some in our church struggled with the idea of providing a casual venue for talking about faith with nonbelievers. They preferred street evangelism and handing out tracts. We were accused of using deceptive methods to share the gospel. In their mind it was a bait-and-switch program.

As we searched for a location for our Lifetree Café, most businesses said no. As soon as we mentioned that it was a church ministry, they seemed to find reasons not to accommodate us. But ultimately, God led us to a man who was willing to lease his café to us one night a week, and it has been exactly where we were meant to be.

In October of 2010, we opened the doors of Lifetree Café. From the first day, our guests have told us they feel comfortable and not threatened. They're eager to talk and to be heard.

The past 17 months have been amazing. Here are just a few examples of the ways God has blessed us through Lifetree Café:

- He's brought many dealing with divorce to us for healing and fellowship.
- He's brought several people with serious or terminal illnesses.
- He's brought families struggling with death, even suicide, in their families.
- He's brought the lonely and hurting.
- He's taught us to care for those who believe differently.
- He's brought witches, new agers, Unitarians, and atheists.
- He's brought women trapped in abuse and even slavery.
- He's helped us to be better listeners.
- He is teaching us how to share our faith in love, without judging.
- He's brought several from our church who originally opposed Lifetree Café.
- He's creating a little church, at Lifetree Café, that now cares for those who would never come to our actual church building.
- He's provided the needed funds for Lifetree Café.
- He's answered countless prayer requests of our Lifetree friends.

We estimate that we've touched over 1,000 lives at Lifetree Café that we would have never encountered otherwise.

Several years ago, I had prayed that God would give me a heart for others. I always loved my friends and family but couldn't transfer that love to those I didn't know. God, through Lifetree Café, has answered my prayer. My favorite night of the week is Lifetree Café night. I wish we could be open every night of the week.

When we started searching for God's leading in 2008, we never imagined what he would have us do. With the help of Lifetree Café, he's changing our church, he's changing our community, and we believe he will bring many people to him who will know Jesus as their Lord and Savior.

Through Lifetree Café, God can change people, he can change lives, and he can change churches.

243

"**LOVE** came through."

Every week Lifetree Cafés from around the country collect comment cards (just as a restaurant might). In this way, we keep our finger on the pulse of Lifetree and, even in the most controversial topics, continually thank God for what he does there. One very controversial episode called "My Son Is Gay" elicited these responses:

- When asked, "Did you grow closer to others?" 92 percent said yes.
- When asked, "Did you experience God?" 92 percent said yes.

Here's a sampling from the hundreds of comments on this episode:

"I truly enjoyed this evening. It's the first time I've been open to talking about my brother and niece, who are both gay. Thank you."

"Nice to feel free to speak one's mind."

"Provoked a lot of deep thoughts."

"This was a very timely topic that was hard for some people to relate to, but love came through."

"A very respectful and helpful conversation about a difficult topic."

"Thought-provoking, complicated. Thanks for facing one of the most controversial topics of our time."

"I really enjoyed the insights from adults. I got to hear things that people my age don't say."

"This was great—very open and honest. I want to become more active in Lifetree."

"It was wonderful to experience real life at church."

In light of research that shows that 91 percent of Americans think Christians are anti-homosexual,[1] it's nothing short of miraculous to read comments like these on such a divisive topic. Regardless of how controversial the issues of the day are, Lifetree tackles them in a biblical, Jesus-centered way. And when we do, God is there, ready to connect with everyone in a fresh way.

"Lifetree is changing the **CULTURE OF OUR CHURCH**."

My biggest worry was that only Christians would come to Lifetree and the church would think it wasn't working. I tried to prepare them by saying, "It will probably be months before new people come," but I was praying that God would let them see early that this thing was going to work. We put up posters and passed out fliers. What really helped was calling the newspaper about our press release. I ended up spending 20 minutes talking to the reporter, who was very interested in Lifetree. The next time, 45 people came—half were from the church and the other half were people I'd never seen before. And every night since then about 45 people have come—and always some are not believers.

We've had God Sightings, too. An atheist named John came once and hasn't missed an episode since. Now he carries a Bible everywhere he goes.

And after taking part in one of our service projects, Teresa started coming to our church and brought her daughter. People in the church helped her find a job, which has worked out very well.

Allyson, another unchurched girl, hasn't missed an episode since she started coming.

And during the "Spiritual but Not Religious" episode, a 75-year-old widow raised her hand and said, "I'm an atheist, but I'm not sure what I believe or why."

What is also amazing is the fact that more people are attending our church's Sunday service—and they don't even come to Lifetree. It's interesting to see the unrelated work together. We aren't working so much to perform; rather, we're trying to engage people with the gospel. And this is striking a bell with me and our congregation.

Lifetree is not only a useful tool/philosophy for reaching the unchurched, but it is also a catalyst for changing the culture of our church from inward looking to outward looking, from being judgmental to being accepting, from being closed to being open.

"I now had a **NEW LEVEL OF RELATIONSHIP.**"

The timeliness of last week's episode, "Living After a Suicide," can only be described as divine…it was timing only God could engineer. It was our fourth week in operation. Because Lifetree episodes are sent to us in monthly Experience Kits, if we'd delayed our opening by a month, we would have missed this episode and the amazing opportunities it gave us to minister to people in pain. God has such perfect timing!

Jimmy, the adult brother of a member of our congregation, committed suicide last summer. Obviously, this loss deeply affected the entire family. The family came to Lifetree for the episode, and I had the privilege of sitting with them. I was incredibly apprehensive about the evening, due to the weight of the topic and the freshness of their pain. But God brought such peace to Jimmy's mother, father, sister, brother, and sister-in-law that night. They were so grateful they'd come, and I felt so blessed to be a part of their healing.

In addition, I had no idea that an elderly member of our congregation had lost his son 8 to 10 years ago to suicide. As this man wept in my arms, I realized that our relationship has reached a new level. We had gone to a place in his soul that most people will never reach.

"I haven't told this **TO ANYONE, EVER.**"

A man at our table said, "I haven't told this to anyone, ever." He told us that his sister had been placed on life support. His parents and siblings wanted to pull the plug, but he didn't. The doctor said that it had to be a family decision. But they did it in spite of his objections. After he finished his story, he said, "I've never been able to tell anyone this—at church or anywhere—because I didn't think they would take it right, but somehow I felt you three could take it. You're the only three people on the planet who know this."

What Those Who Come to Lifetree Café SAY ABOUT THEIR EXPERIENCES

Every week, thousands of people gather at Lifetree Café branches across the country.

Over the years, we've amassed stacks of stories and thousands of comments. Here's a sample of what they've written about Lifetree Café on their comment cards:

"This Lifetree Café is the best thing to happen to this town and myself. I enjoyed it my first time and continue to keep coming. It lifts my spirits."

"I really felt the power of the Holy Spirit here."

"I found my answer. Jesus spoke to me during the presentation."

"I really enjoyed today, and all of the stories gave me chills. It opened my heart to Jesus and to forgiving and loving others again."

"Great atmosphere, friendly people, interesting topic."

"Really emotional and connecting. The Spirit of God was here."

"This has been the most powerful message I've heard."

"Very intense discussion, helpful."

"Just a great topic that made me think about my life and faith."

"Just couldn't help but think of God's words."

"Thanks for being here for us."

"Who wants to be tolerated? I want to be accepted, respected, and included. And that's what I get at Lifetree Café!"

"I really enjoyed the depth of the conversation."

"A very worthwhile and meaningful experience."

"I'm enjoying the people and getting closer to what God wants me to do."

"I've met some very nice people here at Lifetree Café. Thank you!"

"It's great to meet new people. I met two great friends tonight."

"Very thought-provoking and moving."

"Loved the topic and discussion questions. Learned not to judge others."

"You guys are awesome, and the environment is very inviting."

247

"It's pleasant and peaceful and pretty here. A person feels welcome. It's nice to be with people. Also, I felt drawn to this church."

"I really like Lifetree. It lifts my spirit every time I come. I feel that I grow closer and closer to God."

"It struck close to home. I deal with some of the same issues in my family."

"It's amazing how God puts things in your path that he knows you need. This particular topic was touching and closely related to some things I've been dealing with."

"Great tie-in to Scripture about God knowing your thoughts and reasons. What a comfort! This really allowed for open conversation about a tough topic."

"Very encouraging about how we are all unique. God made us to be ourselves, how he wanted us to be according to his plan."

"God works in special ways. My friend made me come tonight, and it was just what I needed, when I needed it!"

"We really like this setting and low-key café feel while talking about God."

We could fill an entire book with heart-warming, jaw-dropping stories like these. It's hard to contain our enthusiasm because we see God do such amazing things each week through Lifetree Café. It's a real-time laboratory of love. It's an environment that uniquely reaches those in our culture who are spiritually open. It is an idea "for such a time as this."

If you're interested in learning more about this exhilarating ministry, check out LifetreeCafe.com.

> "Jesus also did many other things. If they were all written down, I suppose **THE WHOLE WORLD COULD NOT CONTAIN THE BOOKS THAT WOULD BE WRITTEN.**"
>
> — John 21:25

Endnote

1. David Kinnaman and Gabe Lyons, *UnChristian* (Grand Rapids, MI: Baker Books, 2007), 28.

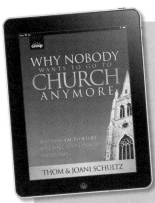

DIVE DEEPER into this book with the enhanced digital version! You'll get videos and links that give you a firsthand understanding of *Why Nobody Wants to Go to Church Anymore: And How 4 Acts of Love Can Make Your Church Irresistible.*

! **Find discussion questions, a forum to share feedback, and more at group.com/4-acts-of-love.**